BUILDING
THE ULTIMATE
MARKETING
AGENCY

BUILDING THE ULTIMATE MARKETING AGENCY

The *Step-by-Step* Guide
to Starting or Growing a
DIGITAL MARKETING
AGENCY

ITAMAR SHAFIR

BMD Publishing

Building the Ultimate Marketing Agency:
The Step-by-Step Guide to Starting or Growing a Digital
Marketing Agency

Copyright © 2022 Itamar Shafir

BMD Publishing
All Rights Reserved

ISBN # 979-8813058738

BMDPublishing@MarketDominationLLC.com
www.MarketDominationLLC.com

BMD Publishing CEO: Seth Greene
Editorial Management: Bruce Corris
Technical Editor & Layout: Kristin Watt

Printed in the United States of America.

Dedication

With feelings of gratitude
To God, the author of my adventure
To my family, my heart and core

TABLE OF CONTENTS

INTRODUCTION

It starts with an idea to become independent, make more money, have more flexibility in life, maybe reinvent yourself.

When I was 21, I was released from my military service, and while studying for the SATs, I began working on a startup called Shark Answers, together with a friend and business partner who was studying with me.

Shark Answers was what Google Answers was in 2001, a marketplace of people asking questions and web-savvy people providing them with answers. We had no business model, but after answering 15,000 questions, we decided to get an investment. For what, we didn't know, but we thought we had a good idea.

We met an investor that wanted to join as a partner. Being older and more entrenched in the business community, he pushed us to start doing secondary research using the internet. It might sound strange to you today, but back then, corporations paid a lot of money to get what we consider today "basic business information".

The company evolved, and we became a secondary research company working mainly for marketing agencies and big brands. We started buying and selling information from the likes of Nielsen, TNS, Thomson and more. But we didn't really make a lot of money.

By this time, I had left college after one semester to pursue my business ambitions.

Since we weren't making hardly the money we wanted, we decided to evolve again, and start providing content-based marketing services, mainly huge amounts of content production for governmental sites, non-profits and brands.

By our sixth year in business the company grew into a full marketing agency. But it was still not very profitable.

Don't get me wrong, I was doing okay, but I was working insanely hard and couldn't see a clear path for meaningful growth.

Fast forward to today, I'm a high-tech entrepreneur with a MarTech exit on my belt, Facebook award winner, a sizeable business, very meaningful income, thousands of businesses I helped build (yes thousands), and the time to invest in projects I'm passionate about while being a full-time CEO.

What happened?

This is not my memoir, it's a guide to helping you start and grow a very lucrative digital marketing agency, without breaking your back, using my very hard-earned experience. Experience not only building my personal agency (the long way), but helping, via Umbrella (umbrellaus.com), to build thousands of marketing agencies.

This book is a guide, a very practical one, that will cut your time to a mid-six-figure agency by 80%.

My goal is to educate as many entrepreneurs as possible about the unparalleled opportunities in the digital marketing industry, and empower them, using this guide, to reach their goals.

THE BEST MARKETERS ON THE PLANET...AND ME

N ow that I've told you a little about me, let me tell you a little about you and what you're going to get out of this book.

What Is This Book?

This book is a guide to building a low to mid-six-figure marketing agency with at least 50% profit margins. It will include proven strategies and tactics.

I read a lot of business books. Often, I find myself sifting through 90% of the book to get 10% I can implement. So, in this book, I'm going to try to make every page a key building block in delivering a strategy or a tactic you'll be able to use as soon as you read it.

You'll find the writing short and to the point, and if I do tell a background story, it will be only where needed.

Who Is This Book For?

It's for people who want or are exploring the option of building a lifestyle marketing agency or a fractional CMO business that makes a few hundred thousand dollars a year with high profit margins. You can absolutely take it from six figures to a seven, eight, even nine-figure agency, but you'll need to read more books for that :-)

The Difference Between a Marketing Agency, Consultant And Fractional CMO

A marketing consultant, sometimes referred to as a fractional CMO, provides consultation, strategy and guidance, but doesn't fulfill the marketing services (i.e., write the copy, deploy the ads or build a website). An agency does both; strategy and actual fulfillment (i.e., getting it done).

In this book you'll learn that you can build an agency with the ability to fulfill any marketing service, but without ever needing to fulfill them yourself. How would that work? Stay tuned.

Is Running a Marketing Business Right for You?

It's easy to answer. Would you enjoy talking with business owners about their business performance, trying to understand what's lacking, and coming up with a plan to solve the problem?

If the answer is yes - then an agency might be right for you. If the answer is no, you can close the book.

Can Anyone Build an Agency?

It is my firm belief that almost anyone who has $10K to invest in their business (buying tools, marketing spend, etc.) and the stamina to learn and get better can succeed.

Having marketing and sales experience will make it easier for you. Lacking that experience will make it harder. Note, when I say HARDER, I mean it will take LONGER, as being good at what you do is, at least partially, a derivative of your experience.

A Book Crafted by Global Marketing Leaders and Thousands of Agencies

I told you this book is going to be to the point, so lesson one, a key aspect in building any business and selling any product is TRUST.

Or in simple terms, why would you listen to me and read THIS BOOK on how to build an agency?

Here is why:

I've given you a brief overview of who I am and what I've done. But my current role, CEO of Umbrella, is the impetus for this book. That job is all about helping people build and grow a digital marketing agency. We've helped many thousands of entrepreneurs over the years.

In addition, in early 2021 I started a podcast called *The Marketing Umbrella* geared toward the same crowd, entrepreneurs building and expanding their marketing agency.

I interviewed and learned from the world's leading marketing experts about ways to build and grow an agency.

At first, to be completely honest, I wanted a book as a calling card, another social proof tool to create authority, but as I interviewed more and more experts, it became clear that this book must be a true GUIDE.

One comprehensive yet simple manual, that anyone can pick up and read, and use the information to start an agency, based on the accumulated experience of thousands of small marketers as well as the leading marketers in the industry.

In this book you'll read specific advice from the like of Neil Patel, Joe Pulizzi, Neil Schafer, Guillaume Moubeche, Mike Roberts, Barry Schwartz, and many others.

This is your formulated path to success.

Steps to Building Your Agency

The easiest way to learn is reading in the same exact chronological order you would need to practice in reality.

Step #1: Branding - social proof, trust, niche, passion, ethics

Step #2: Products & Fulfillment - the services and tech you'll sell, why and to whom

Step #3: Getting clients - prospecting tactics & selling

Step #4: Operations - turning the above three elements into a machine that grows

You will find that each of these steps has many micro steps you'll need to take, but rest assured that completing these steps will build your business.

It bears repeating: The easiest way to learn is reading in the same exact chronological order you would need to practice in reality. (Like a manual)

BUILDING A BRAND

Why is Branding So Important?

Branding answers the question - "Why You?" In a world of many options, potential clients would need a reason to believe your message, to trust you.

Branding = Trust, without which there is no sale.

If you're new to this concept, a good analogy would be dating. Let's say you are quite the catch and have many suitors (good for you :-), and you're looking for that special one.

You'll probably disqualify some suitors if they look raggedy, sleazy, or their overall appearance or demeanor don't meet your standards. These suitors would not even get a chance to date you. They are not in the game.

From the ones you consider suitable and date, you will be looking to "click" a connection, based on time you spend together.

Flipping it to you being the suitor, to get to a point where you actually get a date, you also need to pass step #1. You can't look raggedy or sleazy, and depending on who you're courting, you might need to look and behave in a specific way.

For example, maybe the person you're courting belongs to a different ethnicity or culture and they are looking to date someone from their ethnicity group.

In business that would be the equivalent of a family attorney firm that is looking for a marketer with experience helping legal firms, but you only have experience helping dentists.

In love, never say never, but in business there is no need to fight windmills. It would be much easier to just target dentists and look for a "date" that is looking for you.

So let's start by finding you a business niche.

Task #1: Finding a Niche

There are two main opinions when it comes to niching when starting an agency. One says to niche down, to help differentiate yourself. That is the opinion of the majority of the experts I talk with. The flip side of that is don't niche, because that will open a larger potential market.

Those who agree with niching down are correct, because it builds a brand faster and hyper-focuses your prospecting and self-training. It also allows you to align with your passion or previous experience (more on that later). I spoke with Neil Patel about that on my podcast.

> *"The big issue with small agencies that I've seen is they don't customize their approach. They don't verticalize. Say you're a small agency and you only do it for local businesses that are dentists. You can say, yes, other people can do it, but we specialize in dentists. Look at all the dentists we work with. Here are all the case studies. We know what we're doing, hence we have all these dental clients. You can use another agency, but they don't know how your back-office works, they don't know what an appointment is worth. They're going to go through a lot of the mistakes that we already know."*
> **– Neil Patel**

So, Neil's advice is, if you're small, try to verticalize, try to go niche. That will be your main differentiator, because you know that niche better than anybody else, and client by client, you create an authority in the niche.

You could also potentially target companies that have small, easy-to-manage marketing goals that a newbie could easily deal with. However, those who oppose niching down have a good point in that a niche would have fewer potential clients and might require more specific experience than a generalist who can work with anyone.

Just about everyone agrees that when you're starting up, you take on whoever is willing to pay the rent. But since it's my book, I'm going to recommend niching down to start, and later growing into a generalist that can work with anyone.

How to Find a Niche

The best niche is one you have both a passion for and experience in. For example, you're an avid biker, a semi-professional. It's your passion, and you have some knowledge about the brands, market, prices, players, and most importantly consumer mindset.

If the area you're passionate about doesn't align with what you have experience in, choose an industry in which you have business experience. Perhaps you operated in that industry before as an entrepreneur or an employee. Whatever your experience, you have some insights into the pain points of the players in this market, even if you're not an expert.

For example, if you worked in the mortgage industry, you know the pain points of loan officers, limitations, and budget, so it's easier for you to sell into that industry.

Plus, more often than not, you have a network in that industry that would welcome a marketing conversation and can become your first clients.

If you really don't want to serve an industry you have experience in, then follow your passion.

Maybe you love dogs, and you want to help dog product companies, vets, and pet stores get more clients.

Building a business takes time, stamina, and the road becomes that much easier when you work on a topic that aligns with your passion.

Task #2: Brand Authority

Going back to the dating analogy, how strong a "suitor" you are will be the business equivalent of your BRAND AUTHORITY.

Brand Authority is a culmination of how impressive you are in all facets of your business. How you look (brand appearance), how you sound (the content you produce), your social proof (clients you served and achievements you have like winning an award, writing a book, having a podcast, speaking in major events).

The goal is for your brand authority to be so strong that business comes to you.

Authority builds up as you spend more time in the marketing industry, have more clients, expand your network and develop as a marketer. When you get started, you would need to develop the minimum brand authority required to get small clients.

Personal Brand Concept

The key to branding is differentiation, breaking the noise, not being like the other marketers.

You will see that most of the tasks in the BRANDING section are about making you special, which is in many ways making you different (in a good way) from the competition.

Personal brand concepts are in no way a must, but if you can come up with one, and you feel natural in it (which is key), it will be very helpful to align you with your target audience. A personal brand concept is something in your personality or belief system that can take on a physical manifestation. Here are a few examples:

There is a very acclaimed and talented Sales Coach named Jason Forrest. Jason's demeanor is direct and fearless, and as he trains salespeople, he decided to brand his program the "Sales Warrior". Once that was established, the Warrior branding was utilized in his marketing collateral, conversation, i.e., "We make Sales Warriors, not salespeople" and even in his visuals. For example, in his office you'll see a Samurai Karuta (Armor), katanas, gladiator armor, a spartan helmet and more.

And he makes sure that even on Zoom meetings you have some of these figures in the background. It's all part of a business brand that was born as a personal brand, that fits Jason, and he wears naturally.

A completely different example is Norman "The Beard Guy" Farrar. The name already speaks for itself.

Norm is a super expert eCommerce guy with a focus on Amazon. He helps product owners to brand, market and sell their products on Amazon and other eCom venues.

The depth of experience and success he generated for businesses comes to light in the first conversation you have with him. But before you ever talk with Norm, you already remember him. He has a 15-inch boss-style beard that makes him stand out on stage, in zoom calls and networking events. It is quite different from the scenery.

Norm, being a smart marketer, helps extend the echoes of his beard by adding it to his logo, and as part of his name (Norman "The Beard Guy" Farrar) everywhere. He didn't grow a beard for the brand, the brand came from the beard. It was a natural extension of him.

I'll give you another example, because I know it's hard to think how to implement this for your own brand.

Joe Pullizi is the founder of The Tilt, a community of content creators, and is one of the best-known Content Marketers in the world.

Joe has a dominating color he wears, uses on his swag, logo, and even the charity he founded. It's ORANGE. When he goes on a zoom, podcast, and meetings, that's the color he wears. It's a flashy color, it makes him stand out, and as you see him more and more, you start to associate the color orange with him.

Take some time to think about it. If you don't know yourself well enough, it's time you do. Ask the hard questions like "What are my motivators?" or "What makes me, me?" Enjoy the creative process and create your personal brand.

If you hit a brick wall, no worries, move on. It's not a must to get started or get sales. Your personality will find a way to shine through.

Online Presence

If I'm a potential client, and you reached out to me, odds are I'm going to research you online.

If I look for you online, are you there? Do you have a website? A LinkedIn profile? A Facebook page?

What other online footprints do you have? A Google-my-Business page? A blog? Podcast? YouTube channel? Do you have online reviews? Would I find that you're a guest blogger on different online magazines? Are you a Forbes contributor? Were you interviewed for other podcasts?

When I visit your online venues, would I find out what you do? What about who you work with? Will I see examples of clients you've worked with? Will I see awards you won? Certifications you have?

Ideally, I should find you everywhere, with the best content and achievements, that will make me want to work with you.

> *"Always remember that your present situation is not your final destination. The best is yet to come."*
> **– Zig Ziglar**

As you build your initial online presence, ask yourself - What is the minimum online presence my target audience is expecting, to consider me as a potential partner for their marketing efforts?

This is constantly changing and evolving, but as of the time this book was written, here is what you need to do:

Website

This is a must - a quality website that presents your services, why you are special, WHO YOU WORK WITH (niche), and examples or testimonials of a few clients. (How do you get them when you're starting out? Stay tuned for the answer). If you don't have the budget to build a website and don't know how to build one yourself - you can't really move forward. This should cost you $1,000 tops including design and building.

LinkedIn Profile

This is free, so there's no excuse to not have a good LinkedIn profile. LinkedIn is by far the best B2B social network. Its B2B lead conversion stats are 3x those of Facebook or Twitter. There are many one-page guides online to show you how to set up a professional LinkedIn profile, so we don't need to get to the nitty gritty here.

What is important to mention, and this is true for all your online venues, is the copy. What you write and how you write on your site or any platform, needs to be from the reader's perspective; your potential client.

Be smart and craft the right message, which will be a derivative of the NICHE you're going after, your PERSONAL BRAND and your OFFER (we'll go into details on that in the Products section).

Don't address it as a tedious job you must complete so you can start prospecting. Relish in writing about yourself and your business. Be proud and care about every word. Write, rewrite, and rewrite again as needed. This is your online face. It is you. And on a practical level, good copy will get you more clients, plain and simple.

Have at least 500 connections. Reach out to friends and family, past colleagues, ex-clients, people you meet at events, and of course potential clients you want to connect with.

Getting 5K+ Facebook Likes for Less Than $1K

Depending on your niche, Facebook and Facebook Groups could be more effective than LinkedIn to find clients and colleagues to network with.

In that case, you need a solid Facebook page.

If your agency has 112 fans on your page, it's not very impressive. It needs to be in the thousands. And that's easy to get. For an investment of a few hundred dollars, you can have 5K-10K fans on your business page.

This effective tactic was introduced to me by Facebook maven Kim Walsh Phillips. I tried it myself and it worked very well.

Here is the tactic - word for word directly from my podcast interview with Kim...

Kim Walsh Phillips:

You can actually get Facebook followers very quickly. It's called a promote your page ad, and you can find it right on your business page. You can choose all of the demographics that make a great client of yours. Maybe you're specializing in law firms or health coaches, whatever your niche might be. And then, you want to make the location. You're going to type in this secret hidden option, which is worldwide, and when you type in worldwide, it actually creates this huge audience for you to go after.

And the secret with Facebook is, the bigger you can target, the cheaper it is. So, you'll be able to grow a following that has the right demographics, but maybe isn't the right location. But it will bring that number up, and it will also set up Facebook's algorithm for you because now it's showing these are the types of people that you want to work with. Then, when you place an ad to get clients later on, it has set up the campaign to say, "Oh, okay, now I see that these are the types of people that you want to be able to work with." Now that you put United States on it or Canada or London or wherever you might be located, then you're going to be able to get the clients for your business, and it will be much less expensive.

Itamar Shafir:

That's amazing. When I promote a page, do I need to create a special ad for it or is it kind of an automatic thing by Facebook?

Kim Walsh Phillips:

You do create. They will let you run just with an image of your page. I recommend that you create an ad. You're going to create a quote post because it's something that anybody could like. It should be a motivational quote, five words or less, and you want to make sure it only takes up 20% of the image with the text. The rest should be white space around it. The background should be yellow, the text should be black and you want to keep it so it's super obvious in the newsfeed. You do that so it stands out from a very crowded newsfeed. There's this bright sign in people's way to show them a quote. And then when they like it, they'll like the page."

Review Site

You need a few online reviews/testimonials. Now it's Google-My-Business, but there can also be recommendations on LinkedIn (very powerful), or reviews on your Facebook pages. You can also use those reviews as testimonials on your websites. More on how to get reviews when you get started in the next few pages.

Getting Killer Content in Less Than Two Hours a Week

Once you have a website, and LinkedIn and Facebook pages, you need to create content on a constant basis, gosh darn it.

Generating content on an ongoing basis, especially if you're not accustomed to it, is time consuming, energy draining, and you feel that you're wasting your time because hardly anyone is visiting your online venues (yet).

And it's true, I'd rather have you prospecting and making sales. Luckily, smart people dealing with the same problem already found a way to create content fast.

But before I tell you how, just a word about content creation.

I remind you again, the content you put out, especially when you're a one-man show, is your personal voice.

You MUST treat it with the same respect, preparation and thoughtfulness you would treat what you would say if you were standing on stage and speaking to an audience of your target market. Take pride and joy in it.

I'm reminded of a famous saying attributed to both French philosopher and mathematician Blaise Pascal and Mark Twain. In a letter to a friend he wrote -

I would have written a shorter letter, but I did not have the time.

Don't be the fluff guy/gal.

Doing Content in 20 to 90 Minutes a Week

Earlier I mentioned content marketing guru Joe Pulizzi. He defines a very simple strategy to deal with content creation on a limited time and budget. He says "Focus on one content creation channel," and in his opinion, podcasts are the simplest form. He spends 20 minutes a week creating a five-to-seven-minute podcast on a subject he promotes, and uses this content across his channels.

Time investment
- 30 minutes finding something to talk about
- 10 minutes recording the podcast (talking head style)
- 15 minutes distributing the podcast on iTunes, Spotify, Google Podcasts, YouTube, and website (Can be done by a virtual assistant)
- 20 minutes doing a transcript of the podcast (use Rev.com) and adding it with the YouTube video of the podcast to your site's blog or dedicated section (Also can be done by a VA)

The content creation, if you already have an idea in your head, because you engage with clients throughout the week and read some interesting content, can take 10 to 20 minutes.

You can hire a virtual assistant for $10-$30 (Onlinejobsph.com, Fiverr.com, Upworks.com) to do everything else for you.

What should your podcast be about? Of course, it should be about the NICHE you want to target and how they can grow their business.

NOTE: *You'll need an HD 4K video cam for your podcast or online meetings with clients. If you don't have one as a default on your laptop, it would cost you about $100 to buy one. Logitec is good. Also make sure your background is neat.*

Getting Killer Content While Getting a Client a Week!

Taking up on Joe's tactic, imagine that instead of recording yourself for the podcast, you would be interviewing potential clients in your niche or people who are the center of influence in that area.

As an example, let's say you want to go after CPAs (accountants). Imagine reaching out to accountants you would like to work with and say -

"Hi, we are doing a podcast with leading CPAs in [City]. I would love to get [Mr. CPA] on our show to discuss [something they are experts in]. The podcast would also be

turned into a blog and posted on our Facebook page [we have 10K fans], and we'll also be doing some advertising to get this podcast in front of potential clients in your area."

You accomplish much by doing this -

1. You create valuable content from experts (without creating the content yourself)
2. You gain authority by affiliation (to this known CPA)
3. You get other CPAs wanting to talk to you (everyone wants to beat the competition)
4. You get a chance to engage with a potential client, in a low-pressure environment (the interview) and develop trust

Not every guest on your show will become a client, but some will, others will become referral sources, and some will just provide the good content you need.

***PRO TIP:** The same concept can be applied with writing a PR article instead of a podcast.*

***PRO TIP2:** Remember, whatever content you create (video, audio or text) always repurpose it on your other channels.*

<u>A word about your personal voice:</u>
Many people don't feel comfortable with the written word, and more feel awkward on camera.

You might have this image in your head of the amazing radio talent with the crystal-clear voice, or the charismatic show host who everyone loves. Stop. You are not building a career in radio or TV, you don't need to be that 'talent'. You just need to be the best version of YOU, and your PERSONAL VOICE is actually the attraction to YOU.

Shay Rawbottom, one of the leading LinkedIn video marketers, explained it best in one of our podcast calls:

Shay Rawbottom:
A lot of people in their storytelling on social media and in their marketing and their promotion make the mistake of thinking they need to be extraordinary to get the attention. It's actually the opposite. You need to be ordinary. The more ordinary you are, the more relatable you are, the more people are actually going to come in the door and think, "Oh, wow, this Itamar guy, I actually relate to him. He's talking about his family. He's talking about work life balance.

Maybe you share an experience of hardship in business, getting fired or having a rough exit. So many people can relate to that. That's not extraordinary. You didn't just go climb Mount Everest barefoot like Wim Hof, you're just ordinary, but that's actually more relatable. The storytellers and the influencers out there who try to be larger than life, "Hey, I'm amazing," will actually get less sales because they're less relatable. I say if you feel like you're just a plain Jane, an average Joe, an ordinary person, that's exactly why you should get on camera, because so many people out there are going to relate to you, and they're going to see you from that perspective in these videos you create, and it's actually going to get them in the door to do business in a way that perhaps they never would have been curious about your business before if you didn't connect to them first on that human level."

Itamar Shafir:

What you're saying is be yourself, be the authentic self of you. What tips can you give to bring that out? People can say, "Okay, I'm ordinary, fine, I'll just talk about things," but they still need to be interesting. What does it mean to be authentic? How would that help me?

Shay Rawbottom:

That's a great question. There are a couple different paths people can take, and the reality is, we are all different. I always say for anyone who's new to getting on camera, and you're nervous, you probably don't want to start with trying to be raw and vulnerable, and share all your personal life. I totally understand that can be really overwhelming. Instead, what you can do, and this is something I break down in my program, is just be helpful. Ask yourself this: "What do I know, as an expert in my industry that my target market doesn't know, that would simply just make their lives easier?"

For example, my target market is anyone who needs help starting videos. They don't even know where to start. I could be helpful by making some content. "Here are five tips for writing headlines for your video content," or "Here's the ideal length of a video for the LinkedIn platform," or "Here's how to overcome your fear of getting on camera." These are all things that are going to be valuable to my target market.

So, figure out exactly what it is that keeps your target market up at night. What are the FAQs? What are the frequently asked questions that people are confused about in your industry? Just start knocking down those objections in your video content. When you do that, you start to position yourself as an authority in that space. I don't pitch, I don't ask for anything. I'm just simply giving away free video marketing tips, and at some point, people decide, "It's time for me to do video. Who am I going to go to? Well, of course, Shay, she's already been providing me all this free value on her blog, I'm going to go hit up her and her team, because they know what they're doing."

Something else I've helped a lot of business owners overcome is this misconception that we all need to be professional on LinkedIn. We can't share anything personal there. We've all heard that emotions don't belong in business. But emotions do belong in business. Maybe I'm a little biased because I'm a very emotional woman, and that's my edge. But I think at the end of the day, people do business with people, not businesses.

If you only talk about your business, you're still going to get business. I have clients who are very private, who are very reserved, who work in corporate and have restrictions, who can't overshare or open up and be personal or opinionated, and they do still get business just doing the route I mentioned about being helpful.

However, if you want to really level up your inbound leads, I recommend you get authentic. I recommend you share who you really are and what you really believe in. People buy from people who believe in things, who stand for things. If you look at my content it's not always about marketing. I'll get on there and share my beliefs about things like why I think college is bullshit. I don't worry about all the people who are going to disagree and get offended and say, "Well, actually no Shay, this is my experience."

Using Curation System

There are online platforms that curate content for you from thousands of sources (such as Upcontent.com) which you can filter based on your interest categories, site preferences and more, and just get 10-20 content suggestions per week.

These systems also tell you how engaging this content is, how it's trending, etc. These parameters make it easy for you to choose the content that is best to showcase NOW.

You share the content and write a small comment about it, which can be personal or business oriented. It's a simple way to push content that you know will engage with the least amount of effort.

Scott Rogerson, founder and CEO of UpContent, explained this concept of showcasing content on my podcast:

Scott Rogerson:
How do we organically drive more traffic to these great pieces that we've already created? How do we grow the audience so that when we create the next great piece, there's a lot more

people to look at that and we don't have to wait for the SEO curve to catch up with us? That's where curation came in for us.

We were initially manually going out and finding these articles. We would have Google Alerts that would hit our inboxes. We would have our favorite sources for each client we would go to and see what they put out each day. Read through it, have to get approval internally, have to get approval externally, and then do a lot of copying and pasting to get it into whatever social tool we were utilizing for our clients, whether it's Buffer or HootSuite or HubSpot or what have you. More copying and pasting to get it into an email newsletter. And then, forbid we ever tried to actually get that interesting piece in a "Here's what we're reading" section of the website or something valuable, because that required logging into WP admin and some people were afraid of letting us touch it.

Really, this is taking more time actually than writing the fluffier content. That's not great either, because these are third-party articles. So, is there a way to achieve true curation on a consistent basis, showcasing the authority and thought leadership? We came down to utilizing third-party content to create context for the content that you've created. That's a lot of C's. But that really was the focus of finding these third-party articles that are going to be engaging, going to be valuable for the audience, help to showcase that thought leadership saying, "Hey, you don't have to go out and find this stuff yourself, trust us as your service provider, as your advisor. The best thing is out there about the topics that you care about.

Then, when we put out the original piece, there was a greater audience, because we saw twice the engagement rate on these third-party articles. And then when we actually blended it together, we saw twice the conversions off the original pieces, because the audience is now bigger. That's what necessitated the creation of content, because then we needed to get it efficient and we couldn't find a tool to help us do all those steps efficiently, across different social media, different email marketing, different websites. Every tool we looked at said, "You can do those things, but you have to use our social media sharing tool and our email tool and our CMS to distribute that content." It felt like we were settling on those distribution channels to get great curation. The focus of UpContent is great curation to support whatever stack your agency is using and your client is using without you having to switch between tools.

How to Get Testimonials/Case Studies When You're Starting Your Agency

Scenario #1
Potential clients visit your site, they don't see any proof you did a good job for anyone.
Scenario #2
Potential clients visit your site, they see case studies of how you generated success for businesses just like them.

Hmm...which scenario is more beneficial for you?

Yes, the answer is painfully obvious, and it could be painful to you, as you might not have any case studies or testimonials at this stage.

Buck up, we've got you.

Here is a list of ways to get social proof on your site and into your conversations.

Freebies - you talk with colleagues, friends, family and even your service providers (your dentist, mechanic, lawyer, lawn care company, anyone with a business), and you offer to do something small in exchange for a testimonial.

An example of something small would be writing a PR article about them and boosting it on Facebook, building a landing page, offering a few hours of free consultation, setting up a campaign, designing a deck, or increasing their reviews.

It might cost you a bit in tools/ads/time to deliver, but think of it as the cost of buying social proof and real experience.

Let's say you allow yourself $100 in real spend per client. Imagine having five great case studies and testimonials to add to your site, talk about and refer to, and post on your blog...isn't that worth $500?

Colleagues reach out - In your network you might have some colleagues or even friends and family that own a business or work as manager in a business.

Reach out to them and ask for a testimonial or recommendation. Obviously, they haven't worked with your agency yet, so the recommendation can be about you. For example, "John is great to work with. He is a professional in the true sense of the word. He doesn't take shortcuts and always delivers results."

As you can see, this is pretty vague, but it's a real recommendation from a real professional and can go into your CV just like it can go on your website.

Tell stories - You create a section on your website called CASE STUDIES. Do a one-page case study, a campaign you appreciate in your niche. It can be a large company or small one. You Google "best campaigns in [NICHE]" and you're bound to find something close, or go to the Facebook ad library and do some digging.

You write and post the case studies on the website, for the benefit of visitors that can now learn how to create a successful campaign like company X you chose.

If someone mistakenly thinks you did that campaign, well...

It's very important NOT to claim something that you didn't do, but telling a story always creates an unseen bridge between the story and the storyteller. In this case, the storyteller is you.

Mindset and Conduct

Mindset

The last section in branding is your mindset and conduct, which, again, represent you.

Having the right mindset is critical.

You are building a business to make money, but you can't have that mindset when connecting with potential customers.

Your mindset has to be <u>about the value</u> you can provide to your customers.

> *"When you talk with a potential customer, think how you can generate $100,000 for them. Your income will be an inevitable derivative of your customer's success"*
> **– Yanik Silver, The Evolved Business.**

Yanik elaborated on providing value when we talked on my podcast.

Yanik Silver:
I remember I had written a goal to become a millionaire by age 30. I wrote, "I get rich by enriching others 10X to 100X in return for what people pay me," and so that idea of providing

value is huge. Thinking about that, and not "how do we take as much as possible?" but "how do we provide enough value?" Then the byproduct is just automatically that you're successful, and it changes your framework. Even as an agency owner, if you're thinking about, "Okay, how do I provide 10X in value to my client?" That's a different thing too. I think your questions really create your answers. If I'm constantly thinking about, "How do I create 10X value?" your output is going to be completely different than if you're thinking, "How do I sell this to clients?"

You have to feel like that, and if you can't, are you serving the right clients? Maybe I can't be excited by whatever that client is selling. That's okay. That just means that you have to go back and think about what kind of clients, and that goes back to niching or categorizing, and even this four-letter word, "Who can I fall in love with?" It's almost silly, but it's true. Could you love your clients, and what does that look like? Because if you can't love your clients, then maybe you have the wrong clients. If you're just looking at them as, "This is my $50,000 paycheck. I'll get through it," it might be the wrong client.

Itamar Shafir:
Exactly. I agree with you that it starts initially with you and your mentality. How do you project that when you're thinking about yourself, and you're going through the motion of telling them about themselves? Are you thinking about yourself or are you thinking about them? As you said, your success would be a byproduct of the value you provide to your clients.

Lisa Larter, business strategist and digital marketing expert, helps her clients formulate marketing strategies that support their business goals and objectives. She expanded on that on my podcast.

Lisa Larter:

The founder of a psychology practice called because she needed help with marketing to grow her business. I wanted to know how the business worked. I was looking for what the Heath brothers would call the bright spots. So, I literally made her pull out a calendar and write down her sales for every single day of the year, so I could see what was happening in her business.

I noticed a trend. Every so often there was a day where the sales were over $2,500, but most other days they were way below that. I wanted to understand what happened on those high-revenue days. I learned that on those days they were doing testing, which is a higher-priced item that leads to therapy.

Generic marketing wouldn't have worked for her, but specialized marketing, marketing to schools for kids that need testing, marketing to parents who have kids they want to have tested, marketing to pediatricians' offices that are looking for psychologists specialized in testing, and positioning them as the best-in-class testing service in their city, became a differentiator that allowed them to grow. By understanding what was happening, we developed a strategy that has essentially helped her quadruple her business, and have multiple offices, and multiple clinicians.

By focusing, and really peeling back the layers, and looking at the business, and understanding what is the driver of the business growth, then you can align the marketing. If I just went in, and put a pretty little Band Aid on it, and said, "Oh, you need Facebook, and you need Instagram, and you need Twitter ads, and all that," it wouldn't have worked because we wouldn't have known the right thing to do.

If you conduct yourself as mentioned above, your personal brand will shine and people/clients will be attracted to you, because you will be caring, provide value first, and solve their problems.

Conduct

You are always a PRO. You show up on time for meetings, you look sharp, you're engaged and focus on the person you talk with. You ask questions and really listen to the answers, and when you talk it sounds like you're a partner of the business owner you're helping. You are a TRUSTED ADVISOR.

Section 2

PROVIDING MARKETING SERVICES & TECH (WITHOUT DOING THE WORK YOURSELF)

Introduction to Marketing Solutions

W hy are we jumping to solutions? You might think that since we were discussing Branding, the next logical subject would be prospecting and sales.

However, before you engage with potential clients, you should hone your marketing skills, and more than that, understand the tools in your toolkit, which is also equatible here to solutions you can provide.

As a trusted advisor, your job begins with asking a lot of questions. This is also known as 'Consultative Selling'. You are basically highlighting problems in the client's marketing strategy, sometimes even sales strategy, and you, as an expert, lead the client to the right solution.

This can hardly be done without knowing the main tools in the marketing toolbox.

And while you do not need to be an expert, as you will not be providing the services yourself, you'll need to know what they are, how they work together, and why use one over another.

It might seem daunting, but you'll see it's easy to follow.

An agency's solutions consist of marketing services and software. It's what you sell, what provides value and solves the challenges your clients are facing.

It's your factory, and your core, and usually (without this book ;-) it takes years of experience to deliver quality solutions without fulfilling them yourself.

As such, in this chapter we'll address several key cornerstones in marketing services:

- **THE T&C BUCKETS** - All marketing in one simple explanation
- **FUNNELS** - How marketing solutions work together to produce sales
- **PROVIDING A STRATEGY** - You need a plan for each client
- **SALES CONVERSIONS** - If the solutions are not enticing, sales are hard

- **PROFITS** - If your solutions have low margins, your business won't succeed
- **RETENTION** - If your solutions are low quality, you won't retain clients
- **TIME & FOCUS** - If your solutions are done-for-you, you can focus on growing your business.

IMPORTANT NOTE: This book is not Marketing 101. It is important that you educate yourself about marketing fundamentals and study the marketing strategies in the niche you're targeting. Using this book, you'll be able to focus solely on being the trusted advisor, which will allow you time for learning.

THE T&C BUCKETS - All Marketing in One Explanation

While there are dozens of different marketing services and hundreds of tech solutions (which together can be referred to as Marketing Solutions), they can be simply distilled into two buckets:

- **Things that generate traffic** - Google ads, Facebook ads, SEO, influencer marketing, etc. They entice an audience to take an action, such as visit a website, watch a video, fill out a form, download a white paper, etc.
- **Things that generate conversions** - Website, sales video, interactive form, webinar, eCom store, etc. They are turning a visitor into a lead, and in online sales (eCommerce) turning them into sales.

A very basic example would be Google Ads (Traffic Generators), sending visitors to a Website (Conversion Solution) to be converted to leads or sales.

Solutions from both Traffic & Conversion buckets are utilized as detailed in a **MARKETING STRATEGY**:

Inside a **MARKETING STRATEGY** there might be several **CAMPAIGNS**. A Campaign being a specific marketing tactic (a flower shop might have a yearly marketing strategy that includes ongoing promotions on social networks, sending traffic to its online site, etc.). But it also has a dedicated Marketing Campaign on Valentine's Day, with a dedicated budget, effort and set of marketing solutions utilized.

In a **CAMPAIGN**, different Traffic & Conversions solutions are connected together in a **FUNNEL**, usually using an **Automation system**.

If you're getting a brain twister, don't worry, it's simpler than you think. Let's get back to the Flower Shop example. Valentine's Day is coming, and they decide to do a special promotion – two weeks before they do a PRE-SALE at discount rates – *"Avoid the Valentine's Day Rush, Order Today and have it delivered to your loved one on Valentine's Day!"*

They have a concept for the campaign, and now they need Traffic & Conversion solutions.

They want to go all out, so they are utilizing several <u>Traffic solutions</u> that are hyper local:

- Door Mailers (The flashy signs you find hanging on your doorknob) with a phone number, that if you text, sends you back a link to their online store with a discount.
- Facebook Ads within a five-mile radius from their location, with a discount link to their online store.
- A blast email to their entire client base with a discount link to their online store.

As alluded to above, the <u>Conversion solution</u> is their online store.

When you boil it down, it sounds much simpler: ***The flower store is reaching out to potential clients via mailers, emails and Facebook ads, and sending them to a discounted offer on their online store.***

Sometimes, when we use industry jargon like Strategy, Campaign, and Traffic & Conversions, it sounds overwhelming, but when you put in simple English it becomes clear..

The success of the marketing strategy is **measured by a tracking & reporting solution**, like Google Analytics. We'll get to measuring later, but in the meantime, let's focus on the two buckets – Traffic & Conversions.

If this sounds confusing, don't worry, we're going to simplify it, make it complex again, and simplify it again, so you'll understand it well.

Rundown of All Marketing Services (Mind Bomb)

This is going to stretch your focus and memory, but I promise I will be bringing it back to a simple structure. The process of starting with an overview, drilling down to details, and going back to sub-overviews is core for rapid learning, so trust the process.

Solutions That Generate Traffic

This section will focus on digital marketing but anecdotally include other forms of media to bridge the mind gap for those of you who are less familiar with digital marketing.

All forms of traffic generators are divided into to two groups:

> **Push (Display) Marketing** - Offers that are displayed to the target audience without that audience requesting to receive the promotion. This includes TV commercials, Radio, Facebook, Display, billboards, etc.

> **Pull (Search) Marketing** - Offers the audience is searching for. In the old days it was the Yellow Pages. If you needed a contractor, you would open the phone book to find one. Today we have online directories like Yelp, Expedia, and of course search

engines like Google, where we can search for what we want.

Let's dive into them:

Push (Display) Marketing

Features of the below solutions might change depending on when you read this book.
**The word OFFER used below refers to Offers, Promotions, Brands, Content pieces (lead magnets), etc.

Facebook Advertising - allows you to advertise to the Facebook community using many targeting parameters. It has different ad types to facilitate Awareness to an offer, Traffic to an offer and Lead Ads to generate leads for an offer. Excellent ad platform geared toward 25-plus.

Instagram - part of Facebook, presenting ads based on user profile targeting.

Google Ad Network - while Google is essentially a search ad platform, it has a display platform that is used to retarget users who searched for something specific. Case in point, I searched for red boots. Later when I read an article on my favorite blog site, I might see an ad saying "Get red boots now from BootTown".

YouTube (Google) - Video ads preceding, during, or after the video you're watching. Because it's powered by Google, and Google has a profile on you as a search user (things you've been looking for) and as a YouTube viewer, it is very good at matching the right ad to the right user, resulting in a high converting display platform.

LinkedIn Ads - LinkedIn has many ad types. Ads to get more followers for your page, Lead Ads to generate leads for your business, Click Ads to send you traffic. Like Facebook it knows its audience very well; their business profile, content they post, content they like, and other behavior variables it can measure. But like Facebook, LinkedIn is PUSH advertising, as the user wasn't actively searching for a service or a product when displayed with a matching ad.

LinkedIn Organic Reach-outs - There are many tactics for organic reach-out, from crafting content and sharing it, to direct reach-out to potential customers, to reach-outs in Groups (very powerful) and all the way to LinkedIn automation tools. LinkedIn doesn't approve of automation tools, but they are out there, they are useful, and many companies use them without actually spamming.

TikTok - the same as Facebook. I won't expand, other than it is geared toward a young crowd, and unlike Facebook it has a paid Influencer ad network, meaning you can pay, using TikTok's interface, to an influencer to promote your offer.

Programmatic Display Networks (banners) - You see ads on many different sites, such as online newspapers, that could be images or videos. They are served to the site you're visiting via one of several ad networks. In addition, some larger sites have their own internal banner system.

Mobile Advertising - This refers to ads you'll see when using apps. After you win a trivia game, you see an ad pop up for another type of game, or sometimes an offer you searched for online (coming usually from ad-networks mentioned above).

Native Ads (Sponsored Content) - Ever notice that on some sites, when you're done reading an article, there are more "recommended" articles for you? More often than not, these articles are pushed by a sponsor content platform like Taboola or OutBrain.

Influencer Marketing - On TV you can see a show host or even big movie stars "casually" using branded products (e.g., drinking a Coke or driving a Ford). In online marketing, it's YouTubers, Podcasters, TikTokers and Instagrammers who have an audience in a specific niche (such as Beauty and Style) and are paid to recommend specific products and services. This is very effective.

Social Posting (Related to Influencer Marketing) - You connect with a colleague on LinkedIn or you join a fan page of a company on Facebook. They do a promotional post and you're getting exposed to it. You didn't ask for what they posted, ergo, it's under Push Marketing.

__NOTE RE:__ social/influencer marketing - Though I divided the traffic ecosystem into two buckets, there are of course nuances. Influencer marketing for example is a hybrid model - while the audience is not actively searching for a specific solution, they have opted in, and are very interested to receive information from the influencer. It's like saying, 'I'm *not interested in specific offers from Disney, but I am interested in getting information from Disney on a regular basis.' This is why Influencer marketing is super effective.*

Cold Mass Emailing - The process of building email lists (we'll cover that later) and mass emailing them a specific offer. Sometimes referred to as Spam Mailing. This can be done by mass emailing tools that provide dedicated IP like MailJet or MaroPost.

Cold Direct Emailing - Finding a specific, relevant potential client email and reaching out to them. Use tools like LemList.

Cold Social Reach-outs - You direct-message (DM) a potential client on LinkedIn or Facebook to start a sales conversation. There are great tools to automate this process.

Newsletters or Internal Client Emailing - You send a periodic newsletter or a promotional email to your list or client base. This is critical for generating more revenue from your existing leads and clients. Use systems like AWeber, MailChimp, ActiveCampaign, etc.

Cashback Promotions - Promote a cash-back offer (e.g.,10% cash back with every purchase) via networks like Figg or Groupon. The offer is pushed via a network of participating sites like banks, airlines, etc. (you may have seen them in your bank account)

More Push Advertising You Probably Know - TV ads, Radio ads, Newspaper/magazine ads, billboards, fliers, mailers, blimp ads (yes, it's a thing), posters, in-store signs, and more.

Pull (Search) Traffic Generators

Destination Directories - Yelp, HomeAdvisor, ZocDoc, etc. These are usually sites that have a meaningful reputation as the go-to venue when searching for a specific solution, usually very niched (for restaurants, doctors, travel, etc.).

Paid Search - Google, Bing, Amazon - you search for a product or a service and you get an ad for those products or services. There are many different ad types:

- Pay Per Click - You pay to get clicks to your conversion generator (e.g., website)
- Google Local Ads - Pay Per Result ads to generate calls to a specific number. Used for local businesses.
- Google Shopping Ads - Ads that present a specific product you can buy online. For example, search for "buy socks" and you'll see them.
- Amazon Sponsored Ads - You search for products on Amazon, and many times the first results will be ads of products promoted on Amazon.
- Bing - same as Google.

Organic Search - when users click on an organic search result. To get ample traffic you need to be on the first page of Google. To get there we sell a service called SEO which stands for Search Engine Optimization.

It includes the utilization of many different services:

- Content writing and optimization - Search engines want to present content that is relevant to the search term.
- Listings/linkbacks - Search engines give a higher score to sites that are referred to from other sites that are highly ranked. For example, you write an article on Influencer Marketing which is posted on Search Engine Marketing online magazine and refers back to your Influencer marketing service page.
- Structure optimization - Making the site load fast and be mobile friendly.
- Coding optimization - Meta Tagging and Schema Tagging allows a search engine to easily identify what object they are scanning (article, review, etc.) and what is in the content.

There are many more micro services that require knowhow and tools to promote a site to the top of a search engine.

Online Reviews - You probably won't work with a business that has a two-star ranking on Google, or patron a restaurant that has three stars on Yelp. Generating consistent high-ranking reviews requires review generation tools like Broadly, GradeUs, BirdsEye and others.

While Reviews can be Pushed on a user as part of an ad, in essence users SEARCH for reviews when making their buying decisions.

Referral Program - referral programs are about turning your clients into brand ambassadors, enabling them to profit on referring clients your way. These programs can be powered by any affiliate program (e.g., OSI).

Solutions That Generate Conversions

Websites – an online venue for a business to showcase their business, services, products, team, content. It is a digital representation of their business.

Landing Pages – online venues that are focused on a specific message such as promoting a specific product or a specific lead magnet (Download the Top 5 Diets Report, etc.).

Online Stores (eCommerce) – a website that is dedicated to selling products online.

Facebook/Instagram/LinkedIn, etc. – Your page on designated social networks is like another website, engaging users and turning them into followers, fans, and eventually leads.

Online listings such as Google My Business, Yelp, other directories – These usually get double the traffic from search engines than the average site, as they come up first on searches and they are an extension of the business's digital presence. They turn browsers into visitors of your site, or leads.

Chatbots or Live Chat – When you visit an online venue, you might see an option to chat with a live or automated representative. These are the digital equivalent of a sales rep, mainly used for lead generation and providing information to increase engagement.

On Site Popups – These have different names, such as Engagement Widget, Exit Popups, Light Boxes and more. Essentially, they look like popups with a specific message that are set to activate based on visitor action (such as leaving the site or coming back for the third time), time (15 seconds after the visitor lands on the site/page), or visitor info (visitor is coming from a specific state or a specific campaign). More often than not, you see these popups when trying to leave a site, and are alerted by a message to keep you on site or provide your information.

Webinars – An online live event or presentation that users register for. Billed as educational but really a sales tool. Think about any live event/seminar you've seen. It's the same, just online. Instead of a local real estate seminar, it could be a Las Vegas real estate broker doing a nationwide online webinar for real estate investment opportunities in Vegas, or a Facebook marketing software company doing a webinar on "How Small Business Can Crush Facebook with Less Than $500" and so on.

The Conversion component inevitably will provide information for the action a user can take (Buy this, register for that, leave your info, etc.).

Once you niche, your T&C becomes much more specific, and therefore much easier to learn and implement.

You'll find that a limited number of solutions are usually used in specific niches. As an example, real estate agents are always looking for leads. Mainly seller leads, but also buyer leads. There are several different ways to generate these leads, but overall, your campaign is very focused on becoming very good at providing qualified leads for a good price.

When you work with life-style businesses like restaurants, travel and beauty, marketing tactics will change, and BRANDING will play a bigger role in their marketing.

Funnels

Okay, now we know there are many marketing solutions we can use. There are actually many more niched solutions (e.g., just for real estate agents) we didn't include above but they all fit into the T&C funnel.

They are all cogs in a machine we'll build called a funnel.

In marketing we use the term funnel to describe the prospect's journey from being aware of the offering to lead or sale, going through several stages.

There are more and less detailed funnel structures, but overall, these are the steps –

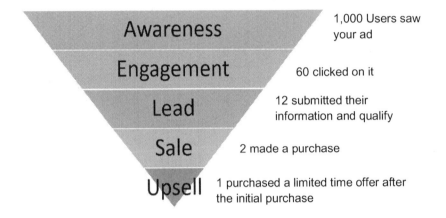

IMPORTANT NOTE: Funnels are tactical plans on how to accomplish specific marketing goals.
Before we can build a funnel, we'll need to create a strategy, which is coming up.

Funnel Examples

Dental Implants Practice

Your client is a high-end dental implants practice. They are focusing on people over the age of 60, with a high household income or a net worth of more than $1 million, in their local community (e.g., Dallas, TX). This would be considered a very small target audience.

You might want to invite people who are 60-plus with a high household income to a live event where they can get all the information about dental implants and ask all the questions. This can also be an online event (webinar).

- You will need a TRAFFIC solution to invite the audience – such as Facebook ads and Mailers.

- You will need a CONVERSION solution to turn them into LEADS and later to CLIENTS. In this example the conversion solution is the live event or webinar.

Below you will find three scenarios for the campaign: one for an Appointment campaign, one for a Webinar campaign and one for a Live Event campaign.

However, you'll notice they all follow the same structure: traffic leading to lead gen, leading to a sales situation (via sales rep or direct online or in event) and follow-up sequence of emails and text messages to support every step of the process.

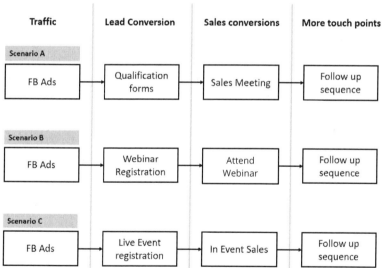

To make this happen, you'll need to get the client branding right (people are not going to show up to an event held by a no-name dentist). Then you will need the following:

- Facebook ad - graphics or preferably quick video ad with the head of the dental practice inviting the audience to an event.

- Landing page - overviewing the event's benefits, why one should come, and of course a way for the audience to register to the event.
- Registration/RSVP mechanism with reminder emails and SMSs.
- Have the event itself set up.

You can outsource all of the above (I'll explain how) and still make very high margins, <u>but the actual plan is up to you</u>.

An easy way to build a funnel is to copy what others have done successfully. As the saying goes "Imitate, then innovate."

Let's take an HVAC example. You'll see it's the same.

HVAC Company Provides AC Repair to Local Homes

If you use Pull marketing (e.g., Google) - you can target everyone that is NOW searching for AC repair. You'll be competing on very costly search phrases, and with leading HVAC companies that have tons of money to spend.

If you use Push marketing (e.g., Facebook), you're essentially trying to convince people that they should repair their AC. Not really the right fit.

But you can find ways around it and entice them to get their <u>AC inspected earlier in the year for a discount</u>.

- You will need a TRAFFIC solution to invite the audience – such as Facebook or Google ads.
- You will need a CONVERSION solution to turn them into LEADS.
- If you're doing search marketing going after users that are NOW searching for AC repair, you want them to land on a relevant page. One that presents the client as the best choice to CALL NOW, CONNECT NOW, CHAT NOW (all the options).
- If you're using Facebook, you need to entice them to become a lead. This is usually done with a promotion, discount, or the like, such as Free AC Inspection During September or 50% off all AC repairs or get your home ready for Winter.

Here's another example: a new cosmetic eCommerce product geared toward young adults. Since it's a new brand, they have no brand equity. No one knows them. So, if you advertise, your conversions will be low. You need to get them SOCIAL PROOF first. One good way to get Social Proof and Traffic is with influencers.

Without getting too much into influencer marketing, you have a lot of Micro Influencers (MIs) that would post a nice usage pic, usage video or shout-out to brands they like just for giving them a free sample. They usually have 5K-10K followers. For a bit bigger MI, you'll pay $500. This would get the right audience + social proof at the same time. Choose the influencer based on their niche (e.g., Cosmetics) and the influence channel based on who they reach. Facebook and Instagram are geared more toward the 25-plus crowd, while TikTok and SnapChat are for the younger audience.

Here's how the funnel would flow:
- It begins with a video post from MIs to their audience, with a limited-time special discount for their community.
- That will lead to the brand's eCom site, specifically to a cart page welcoming that audience and providing the special offer for immediate purchase.
- There will be an exit pop-up if they navigate out as well as retargeting ads for everyone who visited but didn't purchase.

TIP: *It's important to note that TRAFFIC can also come from influencers and business partners. For example, a deal with the local HVAC association can get you in front of a lot of HVAC companies.*

So, when thinking about helping your clients, don't rush into solutions and don't be concerned that you don't know all marketing solutions. Be logical and ask the right questions (coming up in the next chapter). Always think about:

- Who do we go after & why? (The Target Audience)
- Where can we find a lot of them? (Google, FB, Groups, Channel partner, etc.)
- What's the Value we're providing them?
- What's the best way to convince them to work with our client? (Unique Selling Proposition)

In the next chapter we'll learn how to build a strategy without being an experienced marketer. All you have to do is be logical, and attentive to important details which I will lay out for you.

We'll also take a deep dive into how we build a marketing strategy for our clients, even those from industries we may not know. 99% of good marketers hack other funnels as a beginning for their own creative journey. If I need to promote an HVAC, why not look at ads and funnels that other leading companies are doing? More about that coming up.

Strategy

Introduction

You can provide a product, such as Search Engine Optimization (SEO) to get websites highly-ranked in search results. (I'll show you how to provide the best products without doing any fulfillment in the next chapter.)

Or you can go a bit further, become a true marketing advisor and help the business win.
While you can make money with both, the latter is where you'll eventually provide more value, make more money, and have longer relationships with your clients.

But how do you do that?

You need to train yourself. Read books and watch relevant courses. But more than anything, use simple business logic, asking the right questions, and "hack" strategies successful competitors applied.

Let's dive into it.

**Don't forget to niche down. If you do, your journey will be much easier, because you won't need to reinvent the wheel with every new client.*

The process begins with your "Discovery Meeting".
How do you get the most out of that?
Here are the right questions to ask a potential client:

- What is your current marketing strategy and why? What's not working with it? (Now bore into it)
    - How are you currently generating leads?
        - What are you currently doing (or have tried) in traffic? How is it working?
        - What are you currently doing to convert your traffic to leads? How is it working?
- Did you have sales spikes over the last year? Show me. What was it? Why did it happen? (Maybe they have winning products that you can focus on, or maybe they did something that was successful and didn't notice)
- List your top competitors (so you can review what they do well and do better).

- How much money are you spending on traffic?
- What's your connection rate? (How many of the leads you generated turn into a sales conversation?)
  - How many of those do you convert to clients?

These key questions will allow you to understand their current cost per lead, cost for connection and cost of client acquisition.

TIP: Usually, working on just one of these (i.e., leads conversions, connection rate or sales conversions) will increase sales faster.

Crafting a Marketing Campaign Without Key Knowledge in An Industry

So, you had a good day. You had a long discovery conversation with your client, asking the right questions, and after thinking about it, and maybe researching online, you're pretty sure you understand the holes in their marketing. GREAT! That's a really good first step.

Now you need to do something about it.

That can be creating a plan to fix the holes or, in some cases where the business does not have a marketing history you can review, you'll need to decide on the right strategy and tactics for them to start.

Coming again to the rescue, the simple Traffic & Conversion scheme can be used.

- Who do we go after & why? (The Target Audience)
- Where can we find a lot of them? (Google, FB, Groups, Channel partner, etc.)
- What's the best way to convince them to work with our client? (Unique Sales Proposition)

NOTE: Some issues that you'll encounter will be in the business model. A very common one will be a service that is priced too high or too low. Another is a client that wants to sell too many things instead of focusing on their top sellers.

Be on the alert for these potential issues as you do your initial research, asking the client all the questions we mentioned above, and as you run the campaign and see the results.

Legally Stealing Winning Funnels (Competitive Analysis)

The best place to start is to review the funnels of successful competitors. Remember, hacking the funnel is finding the ad (traffic), the conversion units (LPs, forms, sites), and the follow-up funnel (what happens after a lead is generated).

Hacking Google Advertising or SEO Funnels

There are several competitive analysis tools you can use. One of the best-known is a tool called *SpyFu.com*

- using this tool you can actually view all your clients' advertising campaigns: the ads themselves, the copy, what they tried and stopped (i.e., it didn't work), what they have continuously run and are still running (i.e., it works and you should copy).

You can see:
- All the keywords they are going after, meaning when people search for specific words or phrases, such as AC repair, they are shown a specific ad.
- How much money they are spending on Google and how much traffic they generate.

Once you have a couple that you think are good candidates to copy, you can then click on their ads, and see where you land (Landing Page). You can then copy the landing page as well.

Of course, you can't copy word per word. Tweak the copy and restructure it a bit.

Remember, you are doing this to provide your client with a marketing plan. You are not going to do the advertising yourself, or even make the final decisions on keywords. This will be the Google Ads marketer you'll be working with.

Your job is to say to your client – "I think we should do a Google Ads campaign, like your competitor "Mr. Competition," and here is why," and then present what you learned from your research.

You can also search on Google and click on live ads.

I mentioned an incredible tool called SpyFu.com. Mike Roberts is the brain behind it, and he shared how it works when we talked on my podcast.

Mike Roberts:

If you're starting a brand-new campaign, what you can do on SpyFu is figure out who the most effective advertisers are in that niche, and check out their campaign. See which keywords they're buying, and look at their history, every ad they've run, and every split test they ran, and you can effectively determine the winner by looking at which one they kept. Sometimes, for some domains, we'll have 50 tests on a single keyword. So, you can see the results of all that and understand, "Well, what ad copy is going to work?" Ad copy is one of those things that people don't think about a lot because everybody thinks the ad copy they came up with is probably the best ad copy ever written, but in Google Ads, quality score is directly related to what you're going to pay and directly related to the efficiency of your campaign. 90% of quality score is click-through rate. Everything that Google does, everything that Google optimizes for is optimized for effective CPM, which is the amount of money that Google makes per 1,000 impressions. They optimize for that. So, they have this thing that's a quality score, but ultimately the quality score is your click-through rate. It's how much money they're going to make from you. And the only thing that can really impact the click-through rate is the ad copy, so the ad copy is paramount to optimizing your campaign, but also increasing your quality score and driving the efficiency of your campaign.

Hacking Facebook Funnels

Facebook has a section called *facebook.com/ads/library* where you can search for past and active ads by category, keywords and competitor names.

You can see the ad creative (image, video, etc.), the copy, the links that are included, and even related text from the initial funnel, such as questions the advertiser is asking the users once they reach the landing page.

You can and should click on these links and see what the landing pages look like.

TIP: You can also see when an ad was launched and if it's still active. If you're seeing an ad that's been running for two-plus months, it means it's working.

Hack the Entire Funnel

Go through the entire funnel yourself; from ad to conversion to booking an appointment, even talking to the sales rep. This will give you so much more information than just doing an online investigation. You will know their sales pitch and pricing, what emails they send after you book a meeting, whether they send text reminders and what kind, whether a person follows up, if there's a quote form and what's included, and so on.

And again, enjoy it, you are in a creative process.

Case Study Examples

Just Google it :-) I know, it's not really what an expert suggestion should be, but Google is the best way to find small businesses case studies.

I ran this search - "HVAC marketing campaigns case study." That's really straightforward, and I got plenty of case studies.

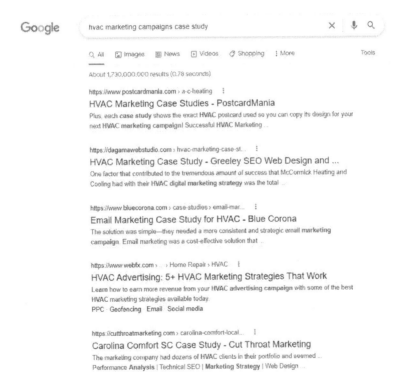

Fulfillment & Delivering Solutions

How to Provide Services Without Fulfilling Them

You have a strategy, a plan for the client, and you get them to sign off on it. Now you need to fulfill and deliver campaigns.

- Maybe you need to build a landing page or several pages in a funnel (aka conversion units)
- Maybe you need to write covering content (aka copy)
- Probably Google or Facebook ads (aka traffic)
- Maybe some automation

What should you do?

Fortunately for you, I'm going to save you a TONNNNNN of time and effort.

You can outsource everything.

> **Option #1** - You search for vendors online, e.g., "white label Facebook advertising services" and you find several. You'll need to talk with them, try them out (they may not be very good), and of course negotiate your wholesale prices.
>
> This requires some work, a learning curve, and low margins to begin with, as you don't have buying

power yet (assuming you're just starting your business).

Option #2 - You plug into Umbrella. Umbrella is my company, so I know all our products and services intimately.

Umbrella provides you one dashboard via which you can resell the leading marketing services and tech you'll need (all done for you 100%). And because Umbrella buys on behalf of many agencies, it gets amazing rates, so you'll always make at least 50% profit margins. Sometimes it's 80-90% profit. Umbrella also provides all the tactical training on how to sell these products with simple videos you can easily follow.

This method has zero searching, sourcing, testing and negotiating, and you can manage all your clients and their products from one dashboard.

Go to www.umbrellaus.com and check it out.

It's critical to remember:
- PROFITS: If your products have low margins, your business won't succeed. When you outsource, you must remember to have at least 35% profit margins.
- RETENTION: If your products are low quality, you won't retain clients. Always work with leading vendors.

- TIME & FOCUS: If your products are done-for-you, you can focus on growing your business.
- PRODUCT USP: If a product doesn't have a specific Unique Selling Proposition, it's harder to sell.

Outsourcing is not ALL OR NOTHING. If you already have marketing experience, and you want to keep some services in-house (such as website building), then just outsource everything else.

Once you plug into Umbrella's platform, you can power any and all marketing services.

Section 3
CLIENT MANAGEMENT

I t's showtime. You are the trusted advisor. Actual fulfillment is done for you, so you can focus on making sure your plan works and managing the client.

When others do fulfillment for you, it might cause you to "forget" about the client and their campaign, especially if it's recurring work like an SEO campaign.

Don't fall into that trap, have bi-weekly meetings with your clients. Depending on the situation you'll use these meetings to:
- Provide more value and deepen the rapport
- Upsell to additional services

Plus, if results are falling behind, these personal touches will keep the client with you as you work toward a positive ROI (Return on Investment).

Tracking & Reports

Reports are for you first. You are the marketer, the planner, the strategist. You need reports to know if the campaign is doing well.

If you use Umbrella, we'll report on every campaign and product you sell. If you use another vendor, demand monthly or in some cases even weekly reports. If you see the campaign is not doing well, investigate with the vendor. Remember some campaigns take time to get ROI positive.

Reporting to Your Client

If your reporting cycle is monthly, make sure you show up with the report every other meeting.

- If it's an SEO report, the goal is to show that you achieved first page on search terms, and an increase in traffic
- If it's an ad report, provide analytics, lead gen numbers, etc.
- If you're in the midst of building a website, provide a progress report.

Reports make clients feel like the process is tracked, and hence, controlled, which translates to peace of mind.

Report Design - Keep it Simple

Reports don't need to be beautiful. Don't overthink it. Get the reports from the vendor and make sure you understand them. Simplify if needed. Then just cut and paste into a deck or doc and convert to PDF.

Let's look at a few real reports.

SEO Campaign Report Example

From left to right: Keywords, First Rank Date (When the ranking was first checked by the SEO provider), First Rank (Where it stood. Notice it says 100. That means it's not in the first 10 pages. It could be on page 11, or page 150), Current Rank (The ranking on that keyword as per the time of the report). Those are the most important details of the report.

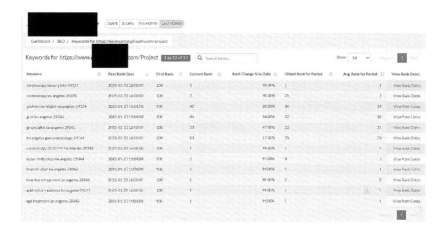

Facebook Ads Campaign Report Example

This is a bit more complex, as Facebook ads require creative approval and allow for potential changes in creative (ad image/video and copy).

- On the left you see the campaign targeting and general parameters.
- In the middle is the actual report for a specific time period. This example is for a lead campaign, so it includes how many saw the ad (people reached),

how many leads were created (main metrics - most important in a lead campaign), how many clicks, and engagement rate (which is important but 95% of clients don't care about anything besides leads in a lead campaign).

- On the right you see the steps of the campaign status: Setup, Ready to Launch (after all was approved by the client, Active (meaning it's running now), and finished, which will be blue as well when the campaign is done.

Section 4
GETTING CLIENTS: PROSPECTING & SALES

Prospecting

Prospecting is the process of finding and engaging with potential clients (not the actual sales conversation).

It takes 16 net hours on average to secure a client when doing manual prospecting, out of which about 80% goes to prospecting.

Prospecting usually involves researching potential clients, reach-out via email, LinkedIn, ads, phone and networking events (in-person or online).

You can reduce the prospecting time by building an inbound lead funnel (hard) or buying leads (easier), but you still need to be ready for the fact that it will take time chasing down leads (people are busy), and it might take several conversations before you have a sale.

That said, 10 good clients and you'll be making more than $100K per year.

<u>The insight here is that</u>
   a) You must learn to pick your clients
   b) You must come up with a process that gets leads to show up for appointments (about 40% show up on average) and get them to work with you ASAP

Picking Clients

When you get started, you can't be too picky. Since this book is geared toward startups and small agencies, we'll focus on how to define the client you want:

- Must have a website - Unless it's a newly established business.
- Must have online reviews - On Google / Facebook / Directory - Unless it's a newly established business.
- In your niche

That's it for when you start up. When you get some clients in, you can become pickier.

Leading with Value / Breaking the Noise

Leading with value means you're not approaching the business with an ask (selling), but rather by giving them something.

Your value can be directly associated with your product or softly connected.

Here are a few examples that have been working very well for some time. You can bank on them.

Softly Connected (But Very Strong) Tactics

[Executive] Lunch / Dinner - You host a meetup of the audience you want. This can be for networking or mastermind. This can also be a virtual meeting. Six to 12 people only. Once you become the host, the person that knows everyone, that is connected to everyone, your potential clients will quickly open to you, you'll learn what's troubling them, and what they need.

The PR Article Tactic - Currently being used in Umbrella's call center to generate thousands of appointments per month. You reach out to businesses, telling them you'll write a free PR article about their business, and promote it online. There is a specific winning way of doing this which I'll detail below.

The Podcast Tactic - same as the PR article tactic, just inviting them to your podcast. It will give you the opportunity to meet potential clients, create rapport (trust) and follow up with a conversation about their business/marketing.

This type of approach is excellent for rapport building. Once there is no "work" to discuss, the client's guard is down, and you can have a truly open discussion with them.

Directly Connected (Also Strong) Tactics

<u>Free Report</u> – For example, Umbrella provides our members with beautiful demand generation reports that provide an overview of the entire marketing status of a client. Sending these reports to clients provides them a lot of value and at the same time positions you as a pro.
See report example in Appendix – Demand Gen Report A

<u>Pay Per Result</u> - You're basically saying to a business you'll partner with them. You want to give them value first, such as get them on the first page of Google, increase their lead conversion rate, or get them clients. They would only be charged after you've done your job.

 Examples:
  – Pay Per Result SEO – We'll get you on the 1st page of Google or you don't pay a dime.
  – We'll 2x-4x your conversions or you don't pay

> *The higher end you go, the more softly connected tactics are used. When you are trying to get clients, you are in the business of creating relationships. This is your sole job, and through the conversations you'll have, you'll learn how you can provide value by asking the right questions.*

Cold Reach vs Referrals

The above examples (networking lunch, podcast, PR article) are reasons to meet and engage. But how do you reach out?

The value proposition is strong enough to do cold reach-outs, but it's always easier to work via referrals. Let's review a few reach-out tactics.

Rapid Network Building (RNB) Tactic

The RNB has been tried and tested by endless entrepreneurs for anything that was sold.

You and your close network of family, friends, current and past colleagues work with a variety of service providers.

I'm not referring to people you know that might have a business or a decision maker in a business. It goes without saying that you should contact them. I'm talking about service providers that work with your personal network.

For example, you or your network might have a dentist you frequent, an attorney or accountant, maybe a car dealership, a veterinarian, or a hairdresser you always go to.

We all have these people in our lives.

Here's what you do: Make a list of 10 people, including friends, family, and close colleagues. Call them and ask each of them to provide you with a list of the service providers they currently work with. Tell them they don't need to refer you or be involved in any way. You just need the name, phone number and email if they have it.

Now you have 50 to 100 people you can call and say - *"Hey I got your number from your client so-and-so. He's my brother/friend/cousin/co-worker etc."*

This puts you in a power position. The person you'll be speaking with would want to be nice to a friend or relative of a client.

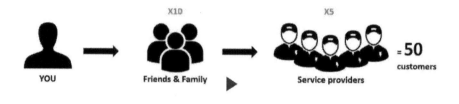

• HVAC/Plumbing	• Pet Care	• Car dealer/repair	• Chiropractor
• Cleaning Services	• Spa/Massage	• Lawyer	• Insurance agent
• Appliance Repair/Handyman	• Lawn care /Landscaping	• Accountant	• Relators
• Pest Solutions	• Taxi/Limo	• Building/contractors	• Gardening services
• Salon Hair/Nails	• Seasonal Sports/Rentals	• Catering	• Other (ask)
• Auto Repair/Detailing	• Therapy (Eye, Mental, Chiropractic, Speech, etc.)	• Florist	
	• Dentists	• Jeweler/Jewelry	

Networking Events and Online Groups

When people see you time and again, and exchange a few conversations, that familiarity is making them much more susceptible to doing business with you.

Many true long-term relationships have their origins in networking events. It's literally all about persistence. People see you and you see them time and again. You both become part of life's scenery (in a good way). By the fourth networking event, they all recognize you, even if you never talked to them.

This is why events, conferences, masterminds, work very well.

No matter which NICHE you want to target, it will have events and small-group masterminds.

They'll also have a digital, less effective version called Facebook and LinkedIn groups. There are networking groups on these networks that have very active discussions and REACH exactly to your audience.

As an example, once upon a time I became a member of the Dentists Professional Network, with 4,749 professionals. I also became a member of the California Retail Network (9,000-plus members) and the Medical Group Management Association (64K members), to name a few.

Can you guess why? I'm obviously not a dentist, nor have I ever been in retail or a healthcare manager. But at some point, the people in these groups were my target audience.

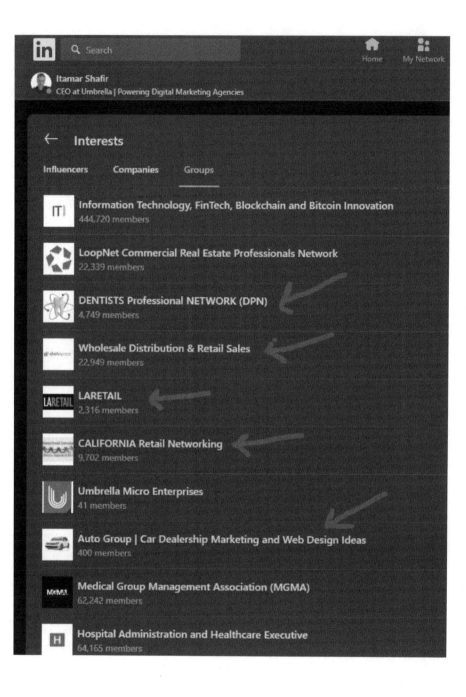

Using The Remora and Magnet Circles Tactic

This tactic was created for real world events, but it also applies to digital groups.

Remora Tactic

When you're starting out, you usually don't have a hefty budget. You may be wondering whether you should get a booth at a trade show, or if you do get one, you're not sure what to do with it.

You need to see what others are doing.

Just about any event you attend will include a booth for a marketing agency or a marketing-related tech solution, such as CRM or Review Generation Software for Dentists (staying with the dentists example).

Much like a Remora fish clings to a shark, feeding on scraps of the fish it devours, you'll be the Marketing Remora :-) circling and clinging to that booth, because it is your lead magnet and qualifier.

Plenty of people will visit the booth. Your job is to target those people and try to find a way to strike up a conversion. That can be as simple as saying, "I saw you were at the "CRM" booth. What did you think about their product?"

When you become a shark, someone else will Remora you. You should enjoy the fact that you've come full circle.

Magnet Circles

Speakers are a point of influence. Many times, you'll find them walking in the crowd, engaging in conversation with people circling them.

JOIN THE CIRCLE. Listen, and jump in if appropriate. Do that time and again with as many influencers as you can. You'll start getting some social proof points just by associating with them, and most people won't have a clue that you don't actually know the influencer. Moreover, you might actually hit it off with an influencer, which will really help you, or you might connect with others in the circle.

<u>Let's bring this tactic into the digital realm</u>
This will also work virtually. Let's say you're a user in a group on LinkedIn, Google, or another platform. There will be many discussions in those groups, and you don't have to be the one that starts them. But when someone does, make sure to comment or reply to them directly along with others who engage with the post. You'll find <u>many of the engagers are potential clients</u>.

Some of them will be influential. They don't have to have millions of followers; they can just be active or well thought-of. This is your opportunity to engage with them over something that has nothing to do with your business. It's like two people meeting at a mutual friend's house, the friend begins talking about how A.I. is affecting businesses, and both of you jump into the conversation and begin talking to each other. This tactic works very well and is a basic tool for social marketing.

The PR Revenue Tactic

This is a lead generation tactic Umbrella has been using in our call center for years to generate many thousands of appointments every month for our members.

This tactic encompasses much of what I mentioned above – leading with value, getting someone's guard down, getting all the information you need from them, and making a consultative sale based on their needs.

You might find this tactic a bit cumbersome. But it's actually a shortcut, and once you follow the steps to the letter, you'll find that you have a winning engine to bring in clients.

Step 1 – Free Value

You contact a business (call or email or direct mail) telling them you're expanding in their area. Offer to write a free PR article about their business, and promote on Facebook for free, if they are willing to provide a good testimonial in exchange. They agree, and you book a time to interview them.

You can make sure they show up to the interview by:

a) Making sure your booking system (such as Calendly) reminders are both email + SMS and it's set to send two reminders day before and three reminders day of.

b) Having someone on your team (VA) call the morning of the meeting and an hour before to confirm they'll be there.

This will reduce your no-shows to almost zero, save you a ton of time and allow you to focus on productive tasks.

Step 2 – The Interview

The interview is in fact a client discovery meeting masquerading as an interview.

We created a script that takes 30-45 minutes to go through. You'll see it in the Resources & Templates section at the end of the book. The questions are interview questions to write the PR article, but they include marketing questions, highlighting potential marketing issues and allowing you to position yourself as a marketer and give more professional free value.

The script is long on purpose. Your job on this call is to create RAPPORT.

- You already provide value by writing the free PR article

- You are providing more value by giving tidbits of consultation during the interview

- You've highlighted their marketing issues

- You've positioned yourself as an expert

All in all, you're creating the rapport you seek. They are buying you. But....

DON'T SELL YET

At this stage, you don't sell or talk about your agency or

your service, other than perhaps alluding to them when talking about your past experience with your clients (if relevant). You'll have time for selling later.

Key point: Book a follow-up call. When you end the interview, you acknowledge their great company, how this article is going to be the bomb and set up a second call to:

a) Review the draft together before it's promoted on Facebook and;

b) Talk about some of the marketing issues that were raised during the interview. Your approach is, "I think you're leaving money on the table..."

If you're not experienced enough to write the article but want to do it yourself, I've provided a PR article template in the Resources & Templates section.

Or, an easy and inexpensive solution is to outsource on Fiverr using our template (see in resource section below) for about $30 per article. It's worth it for those of you who are not quick with the written word.

Step 3 – Second Meeting

You start the call by addressing the draft article. You want to reiterate in the prospect's mind the free value you're providing. You also want the prospect to be aware of your investment, and to acknowledge it has value.

You review it together, get their pointers (if any) and get their kudos by saying things like, "I think you look like a rock star in this article, what do you think?"

Once the article is approved you say it's time to promote it on Facebook.

You boost the article on Facebook for $20, which will get them around 700-1,500 views and some engagement. Create a report from that (see template in resource section).

SALES STAGE

Until now you were the friendly marketing consultant helping with their article. Now it's time to put your game face on and turn into the pro marketer that is going to double their business.

1. You recap all the issues you found on the initial call

2. You add more issues after doing an Audit Report of their marketing status [See example in Resources & Templates]

3. You confirm that they acknowledge these issues, and explain the aggregated loss they create

4. You ask what their goal is, where they would like to be

5. And you chart them the marketing strategy to get there

NOTE: Good audit reports are very impressive when brought into the conversation at the right time. People like to work with pros, and good reports show you are taking every element of their business very seriously.

***NOTE 2:** By this point in the tactic, you are working with the client for all intent and purposes on a marketing objective. You are already their agency, now you just need to take the value you provide and price you charge to the next level.*

Advancing to Dream100 Tactic (Finding Points of Influence)

We've discussed how you prospect directly. But there is another tactic. Instead of trying to connect directly with end clients, you can get people who influence a large pool of potential clients to promote you.

Let's continue with the dentist example. You can create a podcast called Monetizing My Clinic and interview dental supply companies. These companies work with many dentists, and they'll be happy to post the episode you recorded with them on their social network profiles, which will reach your potential clients.

In addition, you'll earn "social proof points" being associated with leading companies in the industry.

Similarly, if you get a chance to speak at a dental event (online or offline), or host one, you'll be reaching a lot of your potential clients with a single focused effort.

Seth Greene is an experienced and successful marketer. Moreover, he helps other people set up a podcast and write a best seller to create meaningful branding and traction for them with a focused effort. This podcast guru shared his insights on my podcast.

Seth Greene:

You want to interview the influencers who can send you who you want. The estate planning attorney has high-net-worth clients who would be great for a financial advisor. But if I walk in the door, cold, and say, "Hey, can you refer me all your clients? Here's my business card," I'm going to get thrown out. I had to come up with a way to build a relationship of trust and confidence to the point where that attorney will say, "Yes, I will. I will promote you to my clients. Thank you for all you're doing for me." It's the absolute best way I've ever found to start a relationship in such a way that the person does not perceive you as selling something or wanting anything. Our close rate on turning guests into clients is incredibly high because they're so warm and fuzzy toward us because we're interviewing them first and promoting them first.

If you're an agency owner, you would start by building a wish list. Who are the top micro influencers in your market? Then reach out to them to be on your show. And not only can you interview your ideal influencers and your referral sources, you can also interview your ideal clients.

And the fact that you can interview pseudo celebrities in your niche, that gives you so much more credibility. Even if you're approaching a "regular prospect". In your case, you've interviewed Neil Patel, you've had, Matt Bacek, you've had some of the household name gurus in the marketing space on your show. Even if you didn't already have all the street cred you have and the history in Umbrella and all that, if you were going to an agency owner, you could say, "Look at who I'm associated with," and hold up that list. Nobody else can do that. It blows any other firm out of the water.

There are many prospecting tactics. The same way we have different campaigns we can offer our clients, marketing our own business is no different.

Scaling Prospecting

Scaling almost always involves forms of paid media. But for some reason, I've seen that many agencies don't use advertising to attract clients. The reasoning is usually one of the following:

1) As marketers, they know they need to build their authority, get the social proof to convert. But they know their brand is not very impressive and predict that as such conversions would be low, which means investing in paid media won't work.
2) They think they are far from fully utilizing their direct and referral marketing approaches (which are free).
3) They don't take the time to invest in themselves (classic case of "the cobbler's sons go barefoot").
4) They don't have a salesperson to support working with a quantity of leads.

The only legitimate reason would be the last one. It's also a very important lesson for when you do campaigns for clients, and something many people ignore.

After you, as a marketer, generate and qualify a lead, and even craft excellent follow-up emails and text messages to get more results from a funnel, you are still only halfway into the funnel.

Now, the funnel needs a sales rep to talk with all these leads, and if you really want success, you also need a sales development representative (SDR) that calls all the leads, gets them to book, rebooks those who don't show, and reminds everyone to come to the meeting.

This part also requires developing a sales script on how to stage commitments from clients, how to down-sell, etc.

Without the sales part working well, the entire funnel breaks, and it will not work for any clients or for you once you decide to scale.

Hence, to scale you need the following:

Advertising – Both Google and Facebook work well for marketing leads. Google has higher intent; Facebook will most likely cost less if you manage to come up with a very enticing offer.

As of 2022, starting with $50 a day on any of them would be enough to have a pretty optimized funnel within six weeks.

Lead Gen and Qualification – An ad leading to a form, or with Facebook, Lead Ads that have forms in them, going to a second qualifying form.

To create landing pages, you'll need a lander system like Unbounce, ClickFunnels, or even a website builder like Wix plus some sort of form solution like Typeform which you will embed in the landers, which will end with a booking app like Calendly or Acuity Scheduling (so leads can book appointments on your calendar).

CRM automation – all the leads (before and after qualification) go into a CRM via Zapier connection. There are three reasons for this:

1. You are able to automate email and text messages follow-ups based on their step in the funnel. (e.g., if they didn't book an appointment, send messages to entice them to book. If they did book, messages that entice them to show up.)
2. So an SDR can call all the leads.
3. So your Sales Reps will have a way to sell.

REMINDER: These are the human components needed to scale:

- *SDR - To call all the leads and get them to book or remind them to show up.*
- *Sales Rep - Hopefully your ads will generate a lot of leads, which means a lot of calls, which means if you don't have time for that or it isn't your strong suit, you need to hire a sales rep or reps.*
- *Sales consultant - To help with scripting, staging, etc. (Unless you're experienced in sales). This is a one-time expense.*

Take into consideration a $20K investment and 2-3 months, including HR and ad budget, plus consulting to get to breakeven and scale beyond to profits.

If you can't get all that in place, you're not in scaling mode yet!

Selling

Client Discovery Call – Consultative Selling

You've got the client on a call, now you need to sell, right? WRONG. Now you need to ask questions!

We touched on some of these earlier, but they're worth repeating. Here are the questions you always need to ask:

- What marketing are you currently doing?

- How is it working out for you?

- What's your cost per lead? Note, this is not always relevant. If it's an eCommerce business, cost per lead is not relevant, instead you would want to know Cost Per Sale, or Cost of Acquisition (CAC).

- What's your conversion rate? (What percentage of leads do you close?) Does one in five leads turn into a sale? One in 10? This is super important as it will give you the CAC for lead-based businesses. Let's say they spend $50 per lead, and close one in 10. That means their CAC is $500.

- What's your product/service's average cost? If they don't have an average, allow them to break it down as they see fit. Let's say for example it's a roofer, and they charge on average $6,000 a job.

- What's your profit margin? (From that roofer's $6,000 job, let's say he makes 30%, which is $1,800).

- What's the Lifetime Value (LTV) of a client? Usually they won't know, so ask, "Ballpark, how many years do clients stay with you? How many orders do they make per year?" (In the case of our roofer, that's not really relevant, since a new roof or a roof repair doesn't happen often. But back to our dentist example, they can easily project the lifetime value of a patient.)

The answers translate to their ROI (Return on Investment). If they spend $500 to make $1,800 in profits, they 3X on their marketing budget - Fantastic! So why do they need help from you?

Many times, once confronted with this calculation, businesses will realize the data they provided is not accurate. The cost per lead might be higher, the closing rate lower. Sometimes they count just the leads they actually connect with, but not the total number of leads. There are numerous other reasons for the inaccuracy.

It could also be that they have reached attrition with this winning channel (e.g., Organic Search) and they need to find other ways to grow.

And of course, in many cases the above calculation will show they simply have a negative ROI.

It could be that the marketing is solid, but their sales guy is bad. Maybe the owner is responsible for sales but is not getting back to half the leads because he is in the field providing service.

Sometimes the answer to positive ROI is business analysis and advice, not even marketing campaign.

Never go straight into SELLING. **Ask smart, logical questions**, and get a solid picture you can work with.

It could be that you'll tell the client you're not sure anything is lacking in their marketing tactics, but their brand doesn't have a strong enough proposition to help them break the noise in the market. It could be their sales process, or follow-up process, in which case you'll need to provide them with business consulting (more on packages and pricing below).

It is important to help clients develop a unique-selling-proposition or brand position, as I recommend you do for yourself.

This is a creative process and as such not easy for everyone. Some people take the highest joy in it, for others dealing with the more tactically aspect of planning and executing campaigns is easier, so it's important that you know you can be successful as a marketing consultant without being super creative. But if you are, it can only help.

A case in point is an interview I did with Matthew Pollard. Matthew is a growth expert, and has several multi-million dollar companies under this belt (don't let that deter you, let it inspire you).

In this interview Matthew exemplifies how sometime just being creative with a business USP can completely explode their business.

Matthew Pollard

I worked with a language tutor years ago. She taught kids and adults Mandarin, and she charged $50 to $80 an hour for private consultation, and she did it successfully. The problem was there were people who were willing to charge $30 to $40 an hour to start their own businesses, and there were people in China offering to do it for $12 an hour on Craigslist, and there was free technology out of Silicon Valley, where you could match up with someone and say, "I'll teach you English, you teach me Mandarin. We just won't charge anyone anything."

So, now she's competing in a hugely commoditized industry, with the lowest commodity being free. She asked me if I could teach her some sales techniques to close more deals. I said, "Sure, but if people are seeing you as a commodity up front, you've already lost. What we need to do is learn how to sidestep the battle altogether."

I went through the hundreds of clients she'd worked with over the years, and I noticed there were two that she helped with more than just language. These were executives being relocated to China.

She also helped them with the difference in rapport in China versus the Western world. In the Western world, if I'm trying to sell you something, at the end of our meeting you'll probably say "Let me think about it." Then if I reach out to you a week later and you still say that, I know my chances of getting that sale are almost gone. Well in China, they're going to want to talk to you maybe five or six times before they even discuss business. They may want to see you drunk over karaoke once or twice. It's the kind of people they are. But they're talking about 25, 50, 100-year deals, not transactional relationships like here. She helped them understand that.

She also helped them understand the difference between eCommerce in China and the Western world, and the importance of respect, where learning the language isn't enough. You have to reduce your accent, how to handle a business card. I said, "Wendy, stop. You're doing so much more for these people than just language." She said she was just trying to help. I said, "Is it fair to assume as a result of the assistance you're giving these people, they're going to be more successful when they get to China?" She said, "Yes, that's the point."

I said, "Great, let's call you the China Success Coach then. Forget about Mandarin education for a second. Let's focus on creating what we call the China Success Intensive." Which worked out to be a five-week program for the executive, the spouse and any children being relocated to China. She loved the idea of this, but wanted to know who she would sell it to. I asked her who she thought she should sell it to, and she said, "Well obviously executives." Basically everybody. Then she said, "Well obviously the companies would pay." In other words, every company that can afford it. Still not very niche. It's like when people say, "I've niched down. I'm only working with small business." I told her, "That's still broad. It's not going to help you. And while they probably have millions of dollars riding on the executive being successful, I still don't feel it's your right fit." She's frustrated now, and asks me, "Well, who then?" I said, "Well, I personally think your ideal client is the immigration attorney." She looked at me like I'm speaking a different language myself.

I said, "Think about it. These people make $5,000 to $7,000 for doing all the paperwork for the visa. I would go to networking events where immigration attorneys hang out. Offer them $3,000 for a simple introduction. They'll love the idea. Double their profit for a simple introduction? When they ask you what they have to say, tell them they just have to say, 'Congratulations, you've now got your visa. I just want to double check. You're ready to go to China?'" The executive would always say something like, "I think we're good. We have our place, we're learning the language, our kids are getting pretty good at it too. We've got our visa. Thank you. I think we're set." The lawyers would just respond with, "There's a lot more to it than that. I think you need to speak to the China Success Coach."

So, Wendy now networks with people that are ecstatic to make more money, and then when she gets on the phone with the executive that's being relocated, or their organization, she has the easiest sell in the world. She charges $30,000 for this five-week program. Minus the $3,000 referral, she makes

$27,000 for the easiest sale in the world. That's rapid growth. And that's the power of what I call having a differentiated and unified message. You've got to get beyond your functional skill. You've got to say, "What are the things I do outside the scope of my functional skill? Either completely unique or unique because of my own experiences, my own background, my own past customers." Everyone has a unique formula that perfectly qualifies them to help a demographic of people.

And then how do I message that? What's the higher-level benefit? Wendy became the China Success Coach. For me, I'm a branding expert, I'm a marketing specialist, I'm a social media strategist. In truth, I'm too many things and nobody cares. But when I say, "I'm the rapid growth guy, and I work exclusively with introverted service providers to obtain rapid growth," the simplicity of that message breaks through that crowded market. It breaks beyond the noise, and creates a rapid growth business. Attach that to even the basic sales process, you get success.

More questions and internal checks:

- Do they have a website? Does it have a strong call for action for users to call or leave their details, submit a quote request, etc.? The form and call for action will change based on the niche.

- Do they have high-ranking fresh reviews on at least one major review site? (Google My Business, Yelp, etc.)

- If they are a lead-based business, are they getting back to the leads? Who is answering the phone and what happens after the call?

Ultimately, all these questions are associated with Traffic and Conversions solutions.

How are they getting in front of potential clients, and in what ways are they converting them to sales?

FUNNEL REMINDER: Simplifying

Remind yourself that no matter what type of business they have or what questions you ask them, their marketing challenges consist of either Traffic or Conversion or both.

And their marketing, *like that of any business on the planet,* is a funnel that is built of several conversion units. Let's review an example again for a business that depends on generating sales via a phone or in-person conversation:

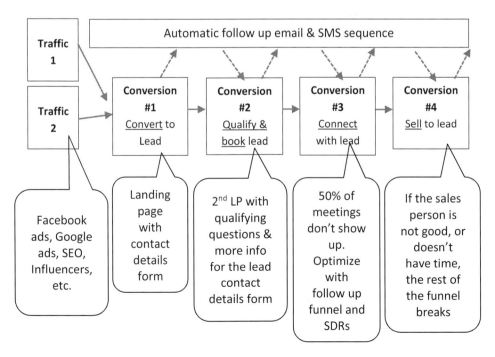

FULFILLMENT REMINDER:

Another important reminder is that fulfillment for the above can be done for you, from traffic-related campaigns to landing page setups and even automation.

It is up to you, as the Trusted Advisor, to understand what in the T&C funnel is not working. This will become second nature after doing several client discoveries calls.

Especially if you're focusing on ONE NICHE, where the clients' offer, funnels and goals are pretty much the same.

Marketing/Sales Plan by Business Type

Any plan you build will use a myriad of traffic and conversion units. As a reminder and a shortcut, I'm listing a few archetypes of marketing plans:

For Lead-Based Businesses

Mainly Home services/Contractors and Professional Services - e.g., HVAC, Garage Door Companies, Roofers, Loan services, Attorneys, Accounting, Dentists, Physicians, etc.

- Solid brand presence – Good-converting site including social proof items such as testimonials, case studies, awards, accreditations, licenses. Good fresh reviews, local listings, website accessibility widget, chatbot.

- Brand positioning - The unique values/position of this specific company. You might need to come up with something. Not a must for all businesses.

- Lead gen funnel (maybe more than one) from different sources. This includes traffic & conversion units but may also include direct lead purchases like leads from HomeAdvisor for contractors.

For eCommerce

This includes businesses that do direct online selling. It might be an e-tailer such as a clothing store, but may also include online courses, software (SaaS mainly), online food orders, ticket and events sales, etc.

If a business wants help growing on Amazon, or any of the main online marketplaces, they will need a specialist. However, if they are a product owner and want to build or expand an independent online store that they want to brand and drive traffic to, you can definitely help. As you'll see, this includes the three listed above, plus one addition.

- Solid brand presence – A good-converting site including social proof items such as testimonials, case studies, awards, accreditations, licenses. Good fresh reviews, local listings, website accessibility widget, chatbot.

- Brand positioning – As above, the unique values/position of this specific company. You might need to come up with something. Not a must for all businesses.

- CPA & Lead-gen funnels - this being an eCom campaign, you want to send traffic to enticing offers. In eCom campaigns we optimize according to cost-per-sale. The funnel includes traffic + special discounts + bundling options + post-sale one-time-offers (upsells) + exit popups to capture info/sales when people are abandoning cart + aggressive follow-up funnels. The plus is that there are no funnel breaks like a salesperson that doesn't call the leads you generate, and as a marketer you have more control over sales. However, it does require a more encompassing funnel.

- Here's the additional need: Influencer marketing is a must for consumer brands. Today even businesses with a tight budget can work with nano and micro influencers to get their offers in front of influencers.

For Brick and Mortars

This includes any business that relies on foot traffic, including offline retailers and restaurants.

Here we need to differentiate between businesses that are more high-end and focus on their brand, and businesses that have commoditized offers and therefore need to focus on limited time promotions.

Being a real-world establishment means you are LOCAL, which means these types of business will usually cater to their hyper-local surroundings.

If they are high-end, like a destination restaurant, patrons will be willing to drive longer and further than if the business is a pizza place (commoditized).

PRO TIP: It is advised, as much as possible, to work with more high-end businesses. They have more money, they value branding, and it's more interesting to work with them.

Perry Marshall has a great book called *80/20 Sales and Marketing*. It's a take-off on the pareto rule that governs that a small percentage of your clients or products will represent most of your revenue.

In his book Perry is taking the 80/20 into everything and anything in sales, marketing and beyond, but I want to mention this approach specifically when choosing clients or prospecting for clients. Knowing your ideal person is knowing your 80/20. Knowing who is your ideal client, will produce very high returns, and hence is worth even a long prospecting cycle.

Perry Marshall:

I don't know anything in business that is more useful than 80/20, and I'm not kidding. I do not know anything in business that is more useful, universally applicable, adaptable to any situation, any context than 80/20. It is the most fundamental law of cause and effect.

80/20 isn't just a little rule of thumb that you write on a post-it note, like 80% of the business is going to come from 20% of the customers. It's not something that you notice in your rearview mirror. It's something that you can predict in advance is going to be true of almost everything you ever do, because it's not this handy dandy formula. It's a law of nature, it's a law of physics, it's a law of cause and effect. The reason is because the world is full of self-reinforcing things like a self-fulfilling prophecy.

Think of it like this. You never want to eat at a restaurant with an empty parking lot. You always want to eat at a restaurant with a full parking lot. Why? Because the full parking lot indicates this must be a good place to eat. People know that, and a crowd attracts a crowd. A stream turns into a creek, which turns into a river because it's self-reinforcing. If the water is flowing down the side of the mountain and it finds this one place to go, it's going to dig deeper wherever it goes. And then all the water is going to go there.

This is how everything in business and in life works. Human beings are basically trained. In school, you want to be a straight-A student because straight A's mean you're equally good at everything. So, you do all your homework and you finish everything on time. Well, in business, if you try to do all your homework, you'll never finish anything. Everything is undone. Everything is incomplete. Everything has dangling participles. In a business, you only have to get an A-plus in one class, and you can flunk all the other ones. But if you pick the right class to get that A, you go supernova.

So, in business you have to figure out what to hyper-focus on and what to ignore. Perfectionism or a straight-A mentality will usually just screw with your head and make you really unproductive. Every Google campaign, every Facebook campaign, every YouTube campaign, every SEO, almost everything inside those things is 80/20 or 90/10 or 95/5. 5% of the keywords get 95% of the traffic. 10% of the ads get 90% of the traffic. 10% of the advertisers get 90% of the visitors. And 10% of the competitors in an industry make 90% of the profit. It is inevitably true, so the easiest way to explain why almost anything works or doesn't work is from an 80/20 perspective.

Offline Retailers

They also need a strong online presence. Suggest that at least some of their leading products be sold online, or at least purchased with a curbside pickup. They also need high-ranking reviews because anyone going to their establishment will check their reviews beforehand.

Local promotions – Discounts on special products, for holidays, for new product releases (Buy one get one, 50% off, bring a friend, join a raffle, etc.).

This system is called HiLo and has been perfected by supermarkets such as Publix, where usually the price is "high" but there is always a set of products that are "low-priced" to attract customers. Unlike EDLP (Every Day Low Prices), perfected by Walmart.

Restaurants

Strong online presence (food is sold in a visual way), plus having a direct takeout solution and a direct book-a-table solution, as well as working with takeout sites.

High ranking reviews with TONS of dish images and atmosphere images.
Restaurants work very well with Micro Influencers that can enjoy a free dinner for their work (making a pic with a shoutout from the restaurant).

Local listing is a must, include them on Google My Business, Yelp and Facebook as well as other leading directories.
If it's a touristy location, make sure they crush reviews on TripAdvisor.

If they cater mainly to nearby workers during lunch and early dinner, make sure they have strong business-lunch menu, as well aggressively priced happy hour.

Assuming the food is solid, the rest is atmosphere, so try to learn the restaurant culture (Young and hip? More conservative? Who are the patrons?) and manifest that on their website, content and even on location promotions.

Suggesting a 'Digestible' Plan of Action

Whatever prospecting and sales tactic you'll be using will end up with a proposal. The right proposal for most small businesses will be $3,000-$5,000 per month for a three-month pilot campaign.

Mind you, I'm not referring to the plan itself, nor the solutions you'll be using that we already reviewed, but rather the scope of the proposal, amount and time, which will make the transaction an easier decision for the client.

A. The price will not be perceived as high.
B. It's time-limited, meaning the <u>client will feel more comfortable knowing the commitment is limited.</u>
C. <u>Milestones need to be reached during that time</u>. For example, a website revamped, Facebook and LinkedIn pages set up, reviews ranking increased, or an SEO campaign started.

Once the three months are up and the client is happy, you'll be able to add more services and increase budget. But whatever your plan is, try to keep the initial proposal around the above boundaries.

Adding a Unique Selling Proposition

There are two types of sales positions you can lead with:

- Product based - e.g., We'll get you on the first page of Google (when selling SEO)
- Value Based - e.g., We'll get you nonstop clients

With both options you'll need a Unique Selling Proposition (USP). This will be something that breaks the noise and creates a differentiation between you and your competition.

Changing Your Offer to Make It Special

Many agencies sell SEO (search engine optimization) services. As we've discussed, those are services that will help a site rank on Google.

Everyone says their SEO is the best. "Look at what we've done, look at the experience we have.".

In many ways, SEO is indeed a commodity when it comes to small-budget businesses, because it's very hard to develop an immersive content experience on a tight budget.

So how do you make it special?

Pricing Model Change

Most SEO services require a monthly retainer with at least a six-month commitment.

You can decide to do "Pay for Performance" SEO and tell your prospective client, "We'll get you on the first page of Google or you don't pay a dime!"

Best In the Niche

Don't say you're the best SEO company, take the niche angle. For example, "We're the leading HVAC SEO company." You could be even more focused: "We're the best SEO Agency for small HVAC companies in Texas."

Or even better – *"We specialize in getting small HVAC companies in Texas on the top position in Google, beating all competition! We can only work with one HVAC company in a service area. Are you looking for more customers? Hire us before your competition does."*

Story Telling (Even If It's Not Yours)

Talking about a story that happened, but maybe not to you.

Mark Hunter is an expert on that, and he shared this story on my podcast:

Mark Hunter:
Building your story isn't easy. Especially if you're a startup, or a small business that doesn't really have any track record, what's the story? Today I was having a conversation with a small company and I shared with them two stories. Not from my own situation, but from other situations I've seen, other retailers and an airline, and it resonated with the person. They said, "Wow, that's interesting," and I said, "Well, this is what we do."

All you're trying to do with storytelling is engage the other person by hooking them with something they can connect to emotionally. If you can do that, then you can begin to get them seeing, "Ah, this is what's possible." Now, if I have a story about me, that's great. But if you're selling to small businesses, do they really care about you? No, they care about them, so you have to be careful of how you frame the story that it doesn't become egotistical, it doesn't become, "I am Superman, I am super human, I can do all things."

Itamar Shafir:
Do you have some tips about how to structure that story? Let's say for example I'm a small agency and I'm going after divorce attorneys. How can I tell that story so it's engaging to that attorney?

Mark Hunter:
Hopefully, you're not sharing your own personal story how you had to hire a divorce attorney. But you can share examples of others. You can talk about the different situations depending on which spouse hires the attorney. "We've seen time and time again that when the female hires the attorney, they have a different level of expectation, especially if there are kids involved. I would imagine, you've had situations as a family divorce attorney involving kids, and that can change very much depending on the ages. I'm curious to know, what are some of the differences that you've seen?"

You can see what I'm doing. I'm crafting a story, and I'm now bringing you into it, by asking you for your opinion.

Now you have to do your homework before going in. But the internet allows us to learn anything and everything. For example, I worked with a small company that taught yoga to corporate employees. I'm not into yoga. But I did some research online, and I talked to some friends who are into yoga, and I was able to set up the story. That's what you do, set up the story and begin to paint. You're holding up a canvas and you have a palette of colors, and you're giving them the brush. You're guiding them to paint the picture. And as they begin to paint, both of you begin to see it. Both of you begin to make changes, and tweak it. Then, when the picture's done, that's the outcome that that potential client is looking for. Boom! Now, I can help them solve their issue.

Value Stacking & Limited-Time Offers

You've seen this many times. It works in every industry. Instead of lowering the price, you add more services/solutions to the offer.

For example, to increase your client's sales, you'll include Facebook advertising and Website optimization and Local Listing and 24/7 AI Sales Bot and monthly reports, along with crafting a campaign, doing the creative (white glove service), and building the automation – all for just $5,000 a month for a three-month pilot. BUT if you close by Friday, it's just $3,997 a month. You save $3K over three months just for closing now!

Minimizing and Upselling

Many of your consultations and strategy plans, especially with very small clients, will get minimized into a series of one-solution purchases.

As an example, you might recommend someone revamp their website to include a better call for action, and to make that pay off for them, you would want to take their reviews ranking up, add an AI Chatbot that would generate leads to the site, make the site accessible to the disabled, run a Google PPC campaign and do content marketing and SEO.

While this is a probably the right strategy, the client might have budget concerns or might want to walk with you before you run together. At that point the plan might be minimized or turned into a series of steps.

First you redo the website. After you do a good job for them, they'll agree to do the review generation. After that works, you do the advertising, etc. This translates to a timeline of review points by the client and opportunities for you to upsell. Which is what I call the Sales Matrix and the Bliss Points.

The Sales Matrix and the Bliss Points

When starting a relationship, in the initial months of delivering the service, you will have very limited credit with the client, and need to reach their BLISS POINT.

BLISS POINT = Meeting their expectations.

The easiest way to do that is starting with solutions that I call "Always Happy" solutions (or almost always).

An Example of an Always Happy Solution is a Website

Creating a website is 100% under your control. You can revise the site until the client is happy with the design and content. This means that you can always make the client happy.

Example of a Not Always Happy Solution
In contrast, a Facebook advertising campaign is a result-oriented solution, meaning the client is expecting to increase sales as a result of the campaign.

Alignment of expectations before a campaign is critical, but still, due to elements beyond your control, such as the client offering and sales team, the result may not make the client HAPPY.

Always Happy	Almost Always	Not Always Happy
Not Result Oriented	Somewhat Result Oriented	Result Oriented
Websites/Landers/ Ecom store	Review Generation	All forms of advertising - Facebook /Google / Display ads, etc.
GMB / LinkedIn / Facebook setups	Email blasts	Regular SEO
Local Listings	Pay Per Result SEO	Podcasts creation

All graphics - mailers, brochures, logos, etc.	Automation services	SDR services
PR – news item or guest blog on major websites	Informative webinars	Sales Webinars
AI / Automated Chatbots		Influencer marketing
Analysis and consulting		

That may be completely NOT YOUR FAULT, but it doesn't matter. They're not happy.

In fact, only a third of advertising campaigns are considered successful by clients.

Taking that into consideration, when starting a relationship, which services would you choose to start with? A website or a Facebook campaign? The answer is clear.

You don't always have a choice, but if you do, be aware of it and utilize it. Even if your marketing plan includes both types of solutions, try to start with the HAPPY ones. Get some credit from the client, before potentially not meeting expectations.

REMINDER: at the end of the day you would want your marketing to be an encompassing 360-degree plan that *helps the client on Branding (the trust side), Traffic and Conversions to leads, and may even go beyond helping with events, training and more.*

This means that every client you start with (if you pick your clients well), can mature into $20K revenue per year on the low end, $50K-$100K on the mid-range and go even higher with bigger clients.

This means building a long-lasting relationship is not a cliché, but a true representation of how you should view your clients for your benefit and theirs.

Section 5
IMPORTANT NOTES FOR THE ROAD

Recap of The Book

You need to find a niche.

Build a brand, and, as much as you can, authority in your domain and niche. This will help you convert prospects to clients.

Start prospecting first with your network, then direct prospecting, and build slowly before scaling with ads.

You can easily manage 10-15 clients making a few hundred thousand dollars a year with direct prospecting before needing to scale into paid media.

When selling, ask the right questions to build a solid plan of action for your prospect.

Lead with value, be earnest and tenacious, and you will build a solid business.

Important Note Regarding Faith

One of my favorite books is Robinson Crusoe by Daniel Defoe. For those of you who haven't read it, it's a must. It is painted as an adventure book, but it's actually a self-growth book and a very intense religious book, where Robinson talks to God time and again. Through tribulations and miraculous luck and fortune, he feels undeserved.

I can't stress enough how much I recommend this book to any entrepreneur or indeed anyone taking a long journey, be it internal or external.

Journeys are not easy. At first, we may be overwhelmed and pushed back by what feels like an uphill battle. Then, we gain some success. A shimmer of hope rises but is extinguished by more hard times.

Finally, we pull through into success, just to feel undeserving.

It is the mere fact we think we're alone which makes us take on the weight of everything in our lives. And though I encourage you to own your failures and success, it is without a speck of doubt that I tell you, we are not alone, and our path is in many ways, guided.

Take solace in that when times are hard, and take care when times are good.

Most of all, take in order to give, and you will shine.

Measuring Success

Many people are unhappy with their current lives, especially entrepreneurs and even successful ones, as they measure their success by comparing their existing life or business situation with an amorphic idea of what success is supposed be.

When you're doing $50K a year, and someone asks you how you would feel if you made $200K a year, you might say "I would feel like a winner", but then you reach that point, and you feel bad because you're not making $1M a year. That means you do not know how to evaluate success (which is common).

In their book The Gap and The Gain, Dan Sullivan and Dr. Benjamin Hardy, analyze this common problem and teach you how to overcome it, which is critical not only for evaluating business success, but being happy in life.

Let me give you the cliff notes gist – Always measure success backwards, meaning looking back (for example, six months) and reviewing your progress. If progress was made as expected, such as hitting your sales milestones, that is success and you will feel happy about it. But if you measure your current situation by comparing it to an ideal, far-away, amorphic goal like "working much less", you will feel like an underachiever.

This works, and moreover, the book explains how to break apart your end goal to more achievable smaller goals and subsequent tasks you can actually achieve and measure.

Big Thanks to Lisa Larter for recommending this book.

Going At It Alone or In Partnership with Umbrella

When setting on this journey, one needs to look at all paths to success.

As an example, a person opening a quick food restaurant, can decide to build their own brand, craft their own menu and plan their own operation cycle, or they can buy into a McDonald's franchise and get all that and more out of the box.

If someone is looking to become a real estate agent, they can go at it alone, build reputation on their limited budget, source leads and learn systems, or they can join a broker like REMAX and be part of a brand that has credibility already.

The same situation lies before you as you start your path as a marketer.

As an Umbrella Member you enjoy several advantages:

- **Fulfillment DFY** – Best marketing solutions Done for You by the leading vendors in the world.
- **High Margins** – 50%-90% profit margins even though you're not doing the work yourself. Umbrella buys on behalf of thousands of agencies so it gets the best prices.

- **Training** – A-Z video training on how to prospect and sell for any marketing solution you want to sell.
- **Marketing Collateral Ready To Go** – Get email swipes, LinkedIn messages, promotional videos, a monthly Umbrella Local magazine you will be able to send to potential and existing clients, and the best demand generation reports in the industry to help you prospect and sell.
- **Branding** – Co-brand with Umbrella Local, our "REMAX" for marketing agencies. Umbrella Local already has countless testimonials and Google Reviews, thousands of followers on LinkedIn and Facebook, leading marketing blog and content creation on an ongoing basis, case studies for all the marketing services, and much more. Being a certified Umbrella Local Expert will give brand credibility Day One. You also get a beautiful marketing website (which you can customize), promotions on our expert directory and blog, as well use of Umbrella Local case studies as your own. So next time someone ask you "what have you done for others?" you can have top case studies to share.
- **Leads Generated For You** – The Umbrella Local team generates quality leads to fill your pipeline with appointments, so you can focus on providing value and selling.
- **Tools to Operate Your Agency** – Get a CRM, billing system, team management, appointment booking solution all included.
- **5 Star Support Team & Ongoing Live Training** events to support your efforts as you grow.
- All managed through one platform.

Having built an agency from the ground up with zero help, I can promise you that working with Umbrella is easier than going solo.

As an Umbrella member you enjoy the benefit of being part of a marketers' community and success-supporting ecosystem, with the flexibility of being your own boss and charting your personal course.

To learn more about Umbrella or book a complimentary consultation, go to:

https://www.umbrellaus.com/

Section 6
EPILOGUE – WHAT MAKES FOR A SUCCESSFUL MARKETER?

O n my podcast *The Marketing Umbrella*, I interview the leading marketers on the planet. Some have agencies, some have marketing tools, some provide marketing or sales training, but they are all successful. They all managed to build a meaningful income independently, in the marketing ecosystem.

On the podcast we talk about ways to help small marketing agencies or people starting an agency in the different domains they are experts on.

I always finish the podcast with a rapid Q&A. I ask everyone the same seven questions. The reason is twofold:
1. I'm interested in repeating patterns
2. The answers provide listeners that are just now starting a business, a clue into how they are like or unlike these successful marketers.

Here is a compilation of their answers:

Did you get along with your parents?	Yes	No	Yes & No
	27	1	5

Do you have a pet?	No	One	Two	3+	Yes
	9	3	6	3	12

When do you wake up? (if an exact hour time is given it is the lower of the two options)	4-5	5-6	6-7	7-8	8-9	9-10	10+
	3	9	10	2	3	4	2

When do you go to sleep? (if an exact hour time is given it is the lower of the two options)	8-9	9-10	10-11	11-12	12+
		5	8	10	10

Are you a man/woman of faith?	Yes	No	Spiritual / Believe in Something	Other
	21	6	5	1

How old were you when your first child was born?	Average
	29.8

Perfect vacation?	Beach	Own property	Any	Adventure/ exotic	Europe
	13	3	6	3	3
	Nature	Cruise	Changes	Disney	snow
	1	1	1	1	1

Here is the list of experts and marketing gurus I interviewed. In addition to the table, you've seen many of their insights throughout this book. When reading about these extremely accomplished individuals, refer back to the table, and remind yourself that we all are more similar than not.

Adil Amarsi is the founder of Copywriting Nerd Ltd and Co-Founder of the Copywriting Mastery Mentoring Program. His clients, who have included Jay Abraham, Dov Baron, and Tony Grebmeier, have made more than $800 million in sales using Adil's advice, copy, and strategies. Adil wrote some of Tony Robbins' highest performing ads while working with Jason Hornung's agency, and he once took a company from $8 million a year in profits to $16 million a year in just six months.

David Asarnow is the CEO at Business Nitrogen and host of The Infinite Business Podcast, in addition to being a business speaker, sales trainer and business growth expert. David built a $45 million new division for a 50-year-old $60 million company over five years. In his 30's he launched a national franchise company that was ranked in Entrepreneur Magazine's Franchise 500 in less than three years and was rated a TOP 15 HOT Franchise in less than five years. David has become the go-to expert for entrepreneurs, executives and small business owners looking to monetize and accelerate their business results.

Matt Bacak is the founder of the EPC Institute and an award-winning Email Marketer. Matt holds the record on Clickbank for the highest gravity ever. His book, "The Ultimate Lead Generation Plan" became a "#1 best seller in just a few short hours using the secret power of leads and big lists. Matt has sent well over a billion emails, done over 8,000 email split test rounds, and his lists are growing by up to 10,978 subscribers a day.

Matt Bailey is the founder of SiteLogic Marketing. He has been hired to teach Google employees to use Google Analytics, consulted with Experian on presenting data, presented search marketing training to Procter & Gamble, and developed online marketing workshops for Microsoft & Orange Telecom. He is one of the highest-rated speakers for his ability to communicate complex information in a practical, humorous way and is the author of Internet Marketing: An Hour a Day, Wired to be Wowed, and Teach New Dogs Old Tricks. With nearly 20 years in the online marketing industry, Matt's impressive consulting roster also includes IBM, Hilton International, Disney, ESPN, Travel Weekly, American Greetings, and The Direct Marketing Association.

Richard Brock is the CEO of SalesTalk Technologies. His first company, Brock Control Systems, was the first CRM company to complete an IPO. His next company, Firstwave, served over 20,000 users in 20 countries. He was named one of the "10 Most Influential People in CRM" by Sales and Marketing Automation Magazine.

Shaun Clark is a co-founder and the CEO of HighLevel, considered the #1 white-label marketing platform for agencies. Prior to HighLevel, Shaun founded, operated, and sold InvoiceSherpa, a SaaS company that continues to help thousands of businesses around the world get paid faster. He has founded several other successful companies, and is considered an expert in all things SaaS.

Melanie Deziel is co-founder and VP of Marketing at The Convoy. She is also a keynote speaker, author, award-winning branded content creator and lifelong storyteller who is on a mission to share the power of compelling and credible content with others. Melanie is also the director of content at Foundation Marketing and the author of the best-selling marketing and business communications book, "The Content Fuel Framework: How to Generate Unlimited Story Ideas." Prior to joining The Convoy, Melanie founded StoryFuel to help teach marketers and creators how to think like journalists and tell better brand stories.

John Lee Dumas is host of the award-winning podcast; Entrepreneurs on Fire. With over 100 million listens of his 3,000-plus episodes, JLD has turned Entrepreneurs on Fire into a media empire that generates over a million listens every month and seven figures of NET annual revenue eight years in a row. His first traditionally published book, The Common Path to Uncommon Success, is the modern-day version of Think and Grow Rich, with a revolutionary 17-step roadmap to financial freedom and fulfillment.

Sean Ellis is an author, keynote speaker, podcast host, and co-founder of GoPractice, Inc. He is considered the founder of the worldwide Growth Hacking movement in which he developed and applied Growth Hacking at companies like Dropbox, Eventbrite, LogMeIn, and Lookout, which led to breakout growth for these companies (all worth billions of dollars today). Sean is also co-author of the book titled "Hacking Growth," and the founder of GrowthHackers.com. His work has been featured in the New York Times, the Wall Street Journal, WIRED, TechCrunch and on MSNBC.

Normal Farrar is the CEO of PRReach, the world's first video press release company, and the President of AMZ Club. He is also an accomplished podcast host and professional speaker. Norm has championed a variety of products and brands to generate sales of over $1 million in sales monthly. Throughout his career, Norm has generated over $100 million in sales between his own products and services and the opportunities he has brokered for clients. He guides individual sellers, brands, and manufacturers to worldwide dominance on Amazon and top-earning sales sites.

Rand Fishkin is co-founder and CEO of Sparktoro, an audience research startup, as well as the founder and former CEO of the marketing software company Moz, and co-founder of Inbound.org. Rand is the author of "Lost and Founder: A Painfully Honest Field Guide to the Startup World." He is a recognized expert on SEO, and is a frequent keynote speaker on marketing and entrepreneurship.

Jason Forrest is the CEO of Forrest Performance Group. He is an award-winning executive, the author of seven books, and the creator of cutting-edge sales and leadership training programs. Jason is the winner of four international Stevie Awards for his Warrior Selling and Leadership Coaching training programs. His book, Leadership Sales Coaching, was named one of Selling Power Magazine's top sales books. Inc. Magazine named FPG as one of the Nation's Best Workplaces for 2017 and Fastest Growing Companies.

Seth Greene is the founder and CEO of Market Domination LLC. He is the only person to be nominated three times for the GKIC Dan Kennedy Marketer of the Year Award. Seth co-hosts the Sharkpreneur podcast with Shark Tank's Kevin Harrington. It was named "One of the Top 10 Podcasts to Listen to" by Nasdaq. Seth is an eight-time best-selling author, and has been interviewed on NBC, CBS, Forbes, INC, and Moneywatch.

Brian Hahn is the founder and CEO of Go Social Experts. He is the author of several books including "The Facebook Formula: How Business Owners Find Big Profits." He created "The Ultimate Facebook Marketing System," which teaches business owners how to profitably use Facebook to market their business. Over the past seven years, Brian has worked with more than 300 businesses in the United States and Canada to develop and implement Facebook marketing systems.

Devin Herz is the founder and Creative Director of Dynamic Marketing Consultants and the author of "ROI Secrets Revealed." He previously ran the lead design and commercial print firm for Quiznos, EXIT Realty Corporate,

Engel & Völkers Corporate, the Tampa Bay Lightning and more. Devin is the creator of InstaVizion and PrintAVizion, two marketing tools that bring video to printed marketing collateral. His company has won two Addy Awards, and Devin also won a Gold Ink Award for design.

Tom Kulzer is the founder and Chief Executive Officer at AWeber, the leading email marketing and automation platform for small businesses. Over the company's 20-year history, Tom has nurtured AWeber from a small start-up to a robust organization that has enabled over one million customers to grow their businesses, and built this impressive company without public or venture funding.

Lisa Larter is the CEO & Founder at Lisa Larter Group. She has been chosen to speak a number of times at the eWomenNetwork International Conference and Business Expo. Lisa is the author of "Pilot to Profit: Navigating Modern Entrepreneurship to Build Your Business Using Online Marketing, Social Media, Content Marketing and Sales." She opened her first retail store, Parlez Wireless, an Authorized TELUS dealership, and sold it in 2012 at great profit

Perry Marshall is the owner of Perry S. Marshall & Associates, and the founder of the Evolution 2.0 Prize. Perry is endorsed in Forbes and INC Magazine, and has authored eight books, including his Google book which laid the foundations for the $100 billion Pay Per Click industry. At London's Royal Society, he announced the world's largest science research challenge, the $10 million

Evolution 2.0 Prize. Perry's reinvention of the Pareto Principle is published in Harvard Business Review.

Guillaume Moubeche is the co-founder and CEO of lemlist, which went from zero to $8 million ARR and more than 10,000 customers worldwide in just three and a half years, without any funding. He is known around the world for helping SaaS businesses, and implementing B2B growth strategies. He has spoken at Join Lion (France), SaaStock local (Belgium), CEED (Slovenia), Touch - Digital Summit (Georgia), and SaaS Nation (Ukraine).

Neil Patel is the co-founder and CMO of Neil Patel Digital. He is a New York Times bestselling author, the Wall Street Journal calls him a top influencer on the web, Forbes says he is one of the top-10 marketers, and Entrepreneur Magazine says he created one of the 100 most brilliant companies. Neil has helped Amazon, Microsoft, Airbnb, Google, Thomson Reuters, Viacom, NBC, Intuit, Zappos, American Greetings, General Motors, and SalesForce grow through marketing. His marketing blog generates over four million visitors per month, with 51% of them spending money on paid ads, and his Marketing School podcast generates over one million listens per month.

Kim Walsh Phillips is the founder of Powerful Professionals, a business coaching and education company. She was recently named No. 475 in the Inc 5000 and is described as an MBA-free, self-made millionaire. She is the best-selling author of multiple books including "The Ultimate Guide to Instagram for Business" and "The No BS Guide to Direct Response Social Media Marketing." She has worked alongside Tony Robbins, Grant Cardone, Kevin O'Leary, Dr. Nido Quebin, Dan Kennedy, Bill Glazer and Gary Vaynerchuk.

Matthew Pollard is the founder and CEO of Rapid Growth, LLC. Matthew is an internationally-recognized consultant, sought-after speaker, best-selling author, blogger, mentor, coach, and serial entrepreneur with five multi-million-dollar business success stories under his belt, all before the age of 30. His client list includes multiple Fortune 500 companies. He was called "the real deal" by Forbes, and his methods have transformed over 3,500 businesses to date.

Ted Prodromou is a LinkedIn Marketing & Sales Navigator Trainer and Certified Business & Executive Coach. He is a five-time best-selling author, including the book, "Ultimate Guide to LinkedIn for Business: How to Get Connected with 150 Million Customers in 10 Minutes." Ted has been called "America's Leading LinkedIn Coach" -- and it's easy to understand why. He has worked with thousands of high-income earners, and before staring his own consulting firm, Ted worked for such companies as IBM, DEC and Cellular One.

Joe Pulizzi Joe Pulizzi is the founder of The Tilt and three other companies, including Content Marketing Institute. He is also co-founder of CEX: Creator Economy Expo. Joe is the Amazon bestselling author of Content Inc., Killing Marketing and Epic Content Marketing, which was named a "Must-Read Business Book" by Fortune Magazine. In 2014, he received the "Lifetime Achievement Award" by the Content Council. Joe also writes fiction, and his novel, The Will to Die, was named Best Suspense Book of 2020 by the National Indie Excellence Awards.

Tal Revivo is the founder and CEO of Adoric.com. He has worked for hundreds of companies worldwide, including Fortune 500 companies such as Toyota, GSK, P&G and Fila. Tal is an entrepreneur, business consultant and designer. He has a wealth of marketing experience, with internet marketing a particular area of expertise. Tal is also an influencer, currently with 219k followers on Instagram.

Mike Roberts is the founder and President of SpyFu. He has led the charge in transforming the way search marketers craft their strategies in PPC and SEO. Mike has consulted such clients as Pinnacle West, NDCHealth, Wells Fargo, Charles Schwab, Meritage Homes, Pulte Homes, Sitewire, TriWest, SAIC, JDA, and Microsoft.

Arlen Robinson is the owner and co-founder of Omnistar Affiliate Software. He hosts the Ecommerce Marketing Podcast, in which he interviews various marketing experts about successful ecommerce marketing strategies, and has produced numerous YouTube Videos on the subjects of ecommerce marketing, SEO and growth hacking. Arlen has also been a part of the creation of numerous successful online guides related to e-commerce, marketing, affiliate programs and more.

Isaac Rudansky is the CEO of AdVenture Media Group. As an educator, Isaac has over 225,000 paying students enrolled in his online courses, and his Google Ads course has been watched by over 950,000 students worldwide. Since founding AdVenture Media in 2013, Isaac and his team have worked with over 500 clients, including Forbes, Hanes, FragranceOutlet, Hearst, AMC Networks, The International Culinary Center, and Agility.

Vincenzo Ruggiero is the CEO of Overloop, with more than 1,000 customers worldwide. They are totally self-funded and have been profitable for more than six years. Vincenzo has also launched five other successful companies and sold three of them.

Neal Schaffer is the Fractional CMO of NealSchaffer.com. He is a popular keynote speaker who has spoken on four continents. Neal is the author of four sales and marketing books, including Maximize Your Social and the recently published The Age of Influence, a ground-breaking book redefining digital influence. He also teaches at Rutgers Business School and the Irish Management Institute.

Barry Schwartz is the CEO of RustyBrick, a New York Web service firm specializing in customized online technology that helps companies decrease costs and increase sales. He is also the founder of the Search Engine Roundtable and is the news editor at Danny Sullivan's Search Engine Land. Barry has provided an advisory role for Google, Yahoo! Search, Microsoft's Bing, along with several other Internet companies and many startups. In 2019, Barry was awarded the Outstanding Community Services Award from Search Engine Land, and in 2018 he was awarded the US Search Awards' "US Search Personality Of The Year."

Yanik Silver is the founder of Maverick1000.com, an author, and the creator of CosmicJournal.com. Yanik's book, "Evolved Enterprise," has been described as a journey for 21st Century entrepreneurs ready to explore how greater purpose, joy and meaningful impact create fierce brand loyalty, marketplace leadership and deliver exceptional profits. Maverick1000 is a global network of successful entrepreneurs with industry-leading companies up to $100 million-plus in annual sales. Yanik has been called a Cosmic Catalyst, a Maverick Mischief-maker and a Galactic Goofball.

Andy Spichal is the founder and Managing Partner of True Online Presence and the founder of Make Each Click Count University. He is also the author of the "Make Each Click Count" book series and the host of the Make Each Click Count Podcast. Andy is a certified dynamic online marketing strategist. He formerly was Director of Web & Marketing at WhatSheBuys.

Joseph Wilkins is the founder of FunnySalesVideos.com and ProCreative Studios. He has created over $50 million in tracked sales and counting. Joseph has written a free e-book on the 8 steps any business needs to do when creating their own funny video with the intent on creating sales. His clients have included Google, LinkedIn, McDonalds, Goldman Sachs, Chevrolet, Discovery Channel and many other global brands.

MARKETING RESOURCES & TEMPLATES

Recommended Reading

The following is a list of books I would recommend for any entrepreneur. They cover key elements about the internal journey, as well business books the deal with different aspects of marketing, sales, time management, and more. The fiction books should be read in full, enjoy them on all levels. The business books can be skimmed through to get to the gist of every chapter (they are tactical tools).

In no particular order:
- Robinson Crusoe by Daniel Defoe – as mentioned previously – the deeper you are in your entrepreneurial journey the more this book will resound and fortify for you.
- The Gap and the Gain by Dan Sullivan and Dr. Benjamin Hardy
- 80/20 of Marketing & Sales by Perry Marshall
- Anna Karenina by Leo Tolstoy – Like Defoe, Tolstoy takes the reader through a journey of several

characters in life, to try and illustrate the positive one. While each character is different, they can also all be represented as different sides of a personality and be interpreted as pathways in their lives.

- The Ultimate Sales Machine by Chet Holmes – a cornerstone business book. Chet wrote this book before the digital marketing age, and while in my opinion it was written more for managers in organizations than entrepreneurs just starting out, it carries existential business truths that you should know – and more than anything else, it's a great project and self-management book which is critical for success.

Appendix – PR Article Interview Script

Interview Script

Introduction section

Hi _____

It's a pleasure to meet you. I'm excited to learn more about your company and write the most enticing PR article for you. Before we begin, just a few words about me and the process today.

My name is _____ and I'm a local Marketing expert with Umbrella Local. My background is in digital marketing and I spend most of my time helping businesses get more sales. Aside from that I'm (add a personal note, maybe something relating you to lead's industry or that you know how it is to be an entrepreneur, etc. – quick 15sec).

This article will be a human-interest story, which means it will focus on you personally in addition to the business. The reason is that people want to work with people they trust.

So, during the interview, be mindful that potential clients will read it, and when you answer the questions, try to include info you think would make them like you and trust you more. Ready to start?

[as you ask them questions, feel free to provide some feedback, and share from your life if relevant, to create rapport]

Let's start with some basic questions:

Full name? Title? (e.g., CEO / Owner)

What's the name of your business? What made you come up with this name? (Keep the answer only if it's interesting)

What service do you provide? (Review their biz beforehand to have some info)

What's the main problem you solve for your customers?

What is the area you cover?

What is your ideal customer persona? (age, gender, has a house/apartment, special interest) I'm asking as we'll promote the article on social networks and we can target specific people for you.

How long have you been in business?

What sets you apart from the competition? In other words, why would people reading this be inclined to hire you over a competitor?

[After they answer, say: As I told you, I'm a marketing expert, and with this article we are trying to help you position your business in the best way. A Unique Selling Proposition, what you might know as a USP and a unique Brand position, is particularly important, not only for this article but for any promotion you will ever do. It is basically the answer to WHY YOU AND NOT SOMEONE ELSE?]

Why did you go into this business? Is there a special story behind it? (Try to find an interesting angle about their passion for this. Or maybe it's a family biz. There's always a reason.)

I see the business is located in _____. Do you also live there? How long? Were you born there? (The more ties we can show to the local community the better effect the article will have).

Are you a big [name of local football team] fan?

How many people work for you? Is there anyone in particular you would like to mention in the article? If so, why?

I did a bit of online research about your business, and found that you have [good/bad/lacking] reviews.

*If reviews are bad, or don't exist, or are very limited, ask: We're writing this story about you, trying to present your business as a leading provider, but you only have X reviews. Why is that? You can get into a one-minute tangent about why reviews are so important.

*If reviews are good, say: I see you have great reviews, how are you getting them? Is it okay if we quote some of the reviews in the article?

What is the most significant event that ever happened to you? (Personal and/or business-related)

What did you learn from it?

If you could share one tip with the readers for choosing a _____, what would it be?

Any other special life events you would like to share?

Do you provide a discount to military folks or other special groups?

Do you personally or via the business support a charity / volunteer?

Are you part of a local business networking group?

Do you have any special awards / certification? (Business or personal)

What's your tag line?

What's your family status? Married? Kids?

What's the best thing you like about [the city where they're located]?

Do you have a hobby?

What's the most unusual job / client interaction you ever had?

Is the business growing? (Don't worry I won't put anything negative into the article.) Whatever their answer, try to understand why and how they might grow faster – provide some free "tangent" consultation. For example, "Did you ever try to do some advertising? Why not? Let me explain how marketing works in 30 seconds." (You have the traffic bucket and conversion bucket... etc.]

Before I forget, I need a good resolution headshot of you or yourself standing in front of your office/truck/sign. If you don't have one, have someone take a picture of you even with a mobile phone, preferably in a bright, naturally lighted room with a clear background. You can also take the picture outside.

In addition, if you have a picture of the team/office that would be great, and your company logo.

*If they don't have a logo, go into the importance of having one (branding, etc.).

Is there anything else you would like to add that you think readers should know? Imagine given the opportunity to talk to many potential buyers, is there anything in addition you want to say to them to get them to LIKE YOU?

I'm a very experienced digital marketing expert. I helped many businesses grow. Since we're already talking, I want to be completely candid with you, as I am with all my clients. You're doing some great things, but you have holes in your marketing that is preventing you from growing your business. These holes can be fixed, which will translate to an increase in sales pretty fast.

With your permission, I would like to send you a free marketing analysis of your business, and schedule another call to review it. On the call I'll show you how I think you can get more sales fast and preserve a long-term growth.

concluding

Okay, great. I'll work on the article and send you a draft as soon as I have one. It shouldn't take more than a week. In the meantime, please email me the pictures, that's very important. And we have another call set for _____.

_____ It was a pleasure talking with you. Talk soon, bye.

Appendix - PR Article Template

Article template

*Note to member: When posting or sending to Umbrella to post the article, make sure to also include under the title, Author: Your Name, as well as a short teaser text to use on Facebook and LinkedIn.

John Treehorn Wants to Paint Everyone in Dallas!

For the past ___ years John Treehorn and his WEBFOOT team of "Seriously Great Painters" have been painting everything in Dallas. Houses, apartments, even kindergartens.

"What makes us different is that

_____

_____ "

John is the owner of WEBFOOT painting, a _____ native, born and raised, and of course a raving _____ fan. John is what we like to call a Local Biz Hero, a self-made entrepreneur who brings true value to his community. High standards of professionalism and strong work ethics of small business owners like John are the infrastructure of _____ economy.

Every dollar that John makes goes back to supporting the local business ecosystem and the community as WEBFOOT supports the _____ charity, as well as doing long term volunteer work with _____.

We sat down with John for a quick interview -
Why do you do what you do?

" _____

_____ "

How did you get into this profession?

" _____

_____ " (include any professional certification, award).

Being a _____ John works directly with many people. We asked him what's the most unusual situation that ever happened to him on the job.

" _____

_____

_____

_____. "

If you could share one tip with the readers for choosing a _____, what would it be?

" _____

_____

_____

_____. "

For those of you who are looking for a professional _____ for any type of work, John and the WEBFOOT team should be your first choice. WEBFOOT supports our troops with 10% discount to military personnel. Call John at 777-777-7777, or visit www.webfoot.com - Seriously Great Painters!

Appendix – Demand Gen Report A (Summary)

Showing the marketing status of a business

Appendix – Demand Gen Report B (Details)

Showing the marketing status of a business

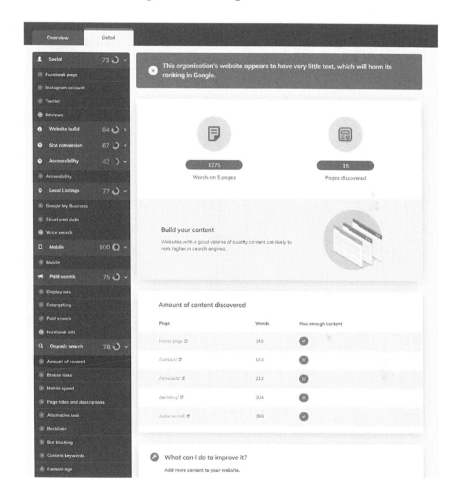

PR Article Report Example

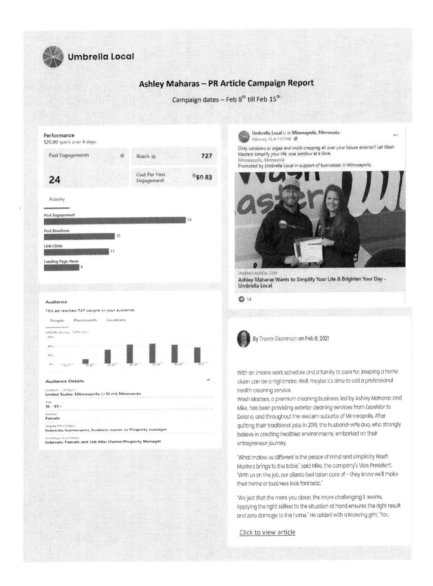

To learn more about Umbrella or book a complimentary consultation, go to:

https://www.umbrellaus.com/

Made in the USA
Middletown, DE
28 September 2022